MW00598347

Character and Conflict

Character and Conflict

The Cornerstones of Screenwriting

Mark Axelrod

HEINEMANN
Portsmouth, NH

Heinemann
A division of Reed Elsevier Inc.
361 Hanover Street
Portsmouth, NH 03801–3912
www.heinemanndrama.com

Offices and agents throughout the world

© 2004 by Mark Axelrod

All rights reserved. No part of this book may be reproduced in any form or
by any electronic or mechanical means, including information storage and
retrieval systems, without permission in writing from the publisher, except
by a reviewer, who may quote brief passages in a review.

Library of Congress Cataloging-in-Publication Data
Axelrod, Mark.
    Character and conflict : the cornerstones of screenwriting / Mark Axelrod.
       p. cm.
    Includes bibliographical references.
    ISBN 0-325-00697-0 (alk. paper)
    1. Motion picture authorship. I. Title.
PN1996.A975 2004
808.2'3—dc22   2004003192

Editor: Lisa A. Barnett
Production: Elizabeth Valway
Typesetter: Reuben Kantor, QEP Design
Cover design: Night & Day Design
Manufacturing: Steve Bernier

Printed in the United States of America on acid-free paper
08 07 06 05 04   VP   1 2 3 4 5

Contents

Introduction: Kind of

This book deals with specific issues concerning two of the most fundamental areas in screenwriting, *character* and *conflict*, and their interrelationship in terms of dramatic potential. To that end, we'll be actively engaged in discussing individual films and in writing exercises that will address these two items which are basic to any screenplay.

As a point of departure in talking about character, let's begin by initiating a *premise;* the word comes from the Latin *praemissus*—"to send before." In other words, it is a statement or assertion that serves as a *basis* for an argument. Every well-constructed screenplay should have a premise and this is closely related to the character's *point of departure,* which I've written about in *Aspects of the Screenplay.* Once you have established a premise, a point of departure, then the proof of the premise, the *point of destination,* becomes that much clearer. The premise initiates the possibility of a predicament and implied in any predicament is *conflict,* so we are beginning to see how a storyline, which evolves out of a premise, is related to conflict.

So how does one come up with a premise? Also, of what does a premise consist? Actually, every good premise is made up of three parts—a *beginning*, a *middle*, and an *end*. Let's use as a premise the "Haste makes waste" cliché and deconstruct it so that we can come up with a kind of storyline.

1. *Haste*—What conclusions can you make using this word? Obviously, the word needs an actor. So who's the actor? Clearly, the first part here relates to an unknown actor or *character* who does something hastily. Who might that character be? In other words, what characteristics can you create about someone who is hasty and what, then, are those things that might be associated with something done hastily? Not coincidentally, this part of the cliché is also the character's *point of departure.*

2. *Makes*—What conclusions can you make about this word? We have a hasty character and a character who is hasty "makes" something. But what is the something the character might make? In other words, what does the word *makes* imply in relation to *haste?* It can imply a number of things, not the least of which could include some *conflict*. But what kind of conflict?

3. *Waste*—The object here is the *point of destination* and that can, in a way, suggest the conclusion to the premise. In other words, a hasty character, as a result of his or her hastiness, makes waste and, implied in the waste created by that haste, conflict occurs.

This notion of premise is used in an attempt to get you to think about how a premise can act as a kind of *blueprint* for the "blueprint" of a screenplay. To that end, let's try an exercise that will prepare you for what's to come.

Exercise

Using what's been discussed so far and the previous cliché as a kind of premise, what can you come up with for a logline? A *logline* is a sentence or two that essentially summarizes the storyline of the entire script.

Try one more—this quote from Oscar Wilde: "Men marry because they are tired; women because they are curious; both are disappointed."

1. Men marry because they are tired.
2. Women marry because they are curious.
3. Both are disappointed.

So, a good premise can be a synopsis for a script in that it offers you a point of departure and a point of destination as well as presenting both the beginning of a *character arc* and at least one conflict.

What's really being discovered here is that a premise can be the *conception*—the kernel of the script. With one, you can begin to organize effectively; without one, you're somehow adrift. With these rudimentary tools to work with, let's discuss something more specific—character.

Character: Some General Principles

Ibsen is known to have once said of his characters: "I have grasped the *leading points* of their characters and their little peculiarities." What's defining about that statement is the attention to detail that Ibsen suggests with the key phrases "leading points" and "little peculiarities." The *leading points* appear to be what Ibsen believed to have been the major traits exhibited by a character; the *little peculiarities* are, of course, the idiosyncrasies exhibited by each character. Taken together these contribute to the overall makeup of the character. But how does one get to that point?

One of the key ways of developing character is through the use of, what I call, *layering* effects. In other words, as you know more and more about the character (his or her leading points and little peculiarities), your character gains substance. The process of layering effects is like adding characteristic details which alter throughout the film because each new conflict initiates a response and that response advances character development. I use the word *layering* as a foundational device; that is, one aspect of a character's character is laid on top of another until, in the end, there is a complete picture of the entire character.

In my previous book, I talked about characters as being *cinelogues*—characters that are real only by virtue of the fact that they exist on the screen; nothing more, nothing less. Even if the script is based on a biography, the character you see on the screen is nothing more than a cinelogue; that is, a tiny measure of who that person may have been in real life and who now is merely a measure of someone else's imagination. Butch and Sundance were not handsome men, neither was Clyde; and Bonnie never looked like Faye Dunaway. The real Rain Man didn't act as well as Dustin Hoffman, and at the end of her life, Isak Dinesen did not look like Meryl Streep.

What we're dealing with in terms of character is *not* character as such, but character as *pastiche*—an image or a semblance of someone real. There's too much complexity in any human being to reduce him or her to two finely edited hours on the big or even the small screen. But characters, because they are a semblance of something real, need to be based on things that are real. So what you have to do as a screenwriter is to create characters (and especially hero–protagonists) that *appear* real to the point that an audience can relate to them. By simplifying the complexity of any one individual character, you can achieve that.

Many film characterizations fail because the writer tries to make characters too *complex* and in the face of that impossible task tends to lose the relative simplicity of the characters. The writer attempts to make them appear more like *real* humans instead of *fictional* ones, instead of cinelogues. So, how does one create cinelogues that are substantially real enough to be convincing? Here's where Ibsen comes in.

Clearly, there are several areas you need to address as you attempt to individualize characters, to get to their leading points and peculiarities. Of those, it is possible to create several categories that include, but are not limited to, heredity, social milieu, and psychological milieu. Each of these includes the following:

Heredity

Sex
Age
Height and weight
Color of hair, eyes, and skin
Physical characteristics and/or defects

Social milieu

Social class
Occupation
Education
Family makeup
Intellect
Religion (or lack of it)
Race
Ethnicity
Political preference
Hobbies
Sexual preference
Abuse (or lack of it)
Drug addiction (or lack of it)

Psychological milieu

Worldview
Disappointments
Temperament
Complexes
Abilities

So what has been created at this point? By using these (and other) characteristics, we can create a character, or at least the outline of a character, that can be developed further.

Now, a premise has been established; that is, a point of departure, a possible point of destination, and the outline of a character. Still there's something missing and that something is dramatic *conflict*.

The German philosopher Hegel is said to have written that "contradiction is the power that moves things" therefore contradiction enhances the storyline. Life is in a constant state of flux and implied in change is *contradiction,* which literally means "to speak against."

Hegel also wrote: "It is only because a thing contains a contradiction within itself that it moves and acquires impulse and activity. That is the process of all motion and all development." So Hegel would probably have made a great screenwriter if he hadn't spent so much of his time philosophizing. But how, then, does character alter? According to Egri, the author of *The Art of Dramatic Writing:*

> A character stands revealed through conflict; conflict begins with a decision; a decision is made because of the premise of the play. The character's decision necessarily sets in motion another decision, from his adversary. And it is these decisions, one resulting from the other, which propel the play to its ultimate destination: the proving of the premise. (1972, 63)

This growth of character is tantamount to what I've talked about in *Aspects of the Screenplay* concerning the *arc* of the character—that is, "that range of *development* from the beginning of the script to its conclusion in which the character alters his or her being."

What is soon discovered when dealing with character is that the development of the hero–protagonist is effective in screenwriting in proportion to how clearly his or her motivation is in conflict with internal and/or external obstacles. In other words, there is a *dynamic quest* at work and it really is the character's quest to overcome those obstacles that we're dealing with when we talk about character *development.*

The word *hero* has Greek origins and, depending on how one uses it, refers to any person *admired* for his or her qualities or achievements and regarded as an *ideal model.* Interestingly enough, the term *protagonist* also comes from Greek, *protos*—first—and *agonistes*—actor. Quite simply, it means the *leading* character or actor around whom the action centers. So the inter-relationship between the hero and the protagonist is a signifi-cant one and one that will be important throughout our work on character development.

This book discusses a number of films, which have been chosen on the basis of what they offer in terms of character devel-opment or lack of it. That is, how a hero–protagonist succeeds or fails as a character. For me, the relationship between *plot* (Aristotle's orderly arrangement of incidents) and *character* can-not be disassociated. In other words, regardless of the relative simplicity or complexity of a plot, the hero–protagonist must go through a self-altering process of some kind and that self-altering process is likened to a *quest*—something sought for or the act of seeking—or a *rite of passage.* So, undeniably intertwined are the relationships between

1. The hero–protagonist (i.e., she or he around whom the action centers)
2. The quest (i.e., that which is sought after)
3. The conflict (i.e., those obstacles that alter the status quo)

As a matter of fact, if you can keep those three items in mind while writing any screenplay, you will stay on target in relation to character and storyline development.

To that end, I'm going to describe Joseph Campbell's approach to the quest and use specific examples of his to show

how various films have used those patterns, consciously or unconsciously, in terms of developing character. Then from there, I will get into specific case studies using the films *Good Will Hunting, Driven,* and *Amélie.*

Before turning to Campbell, I'd like to begin with an idea advanced by David Dortort who not only taught at UCLA and contributed to a number of screenplays during the 1950s but is best known for producing the *Bonanza* television series. Dortort, like Campbell, categorized heroes according to certain archetypes. This idea is not new, but he did organize archetypes into a useful scheme for screenwriters.

According to Dortort, film people dismissed the business of story writing by asserting that there were only five or nine or thirty-seven basic stories and, because of that, everything had been done. Unfortunately, there is no agreement on what the *master* narratives are, even though films have been studied endlessly by genre, style, social content, and other analytical approaches. Dortort suggests that since screenwriters resist complex narrative theories what they need is an overall sense of where the story idea seems to be heading. Knowing a story's general direction (the point of departure discussed earlier) would make it easier to figure out what needs to be said in the story.

Over time, Dortort noticed that the stories pitched his way tended to sort into one of six archetypal categories—the Hero, the Buddy/Friendship, the Impossible Quest, the Breaking-Away, the Medea, and the Faust (Lucey 1996, 24–25). Interestingly enough, these six archetypes have major similarities to Campbell's quest approach and we'll see how they can be integrated to give you a better sense of where you might want to go with your characters.

Lucey in his *Story Sense* also notes:

In European culture, hero stories are modeled after the myth of Theseus, who sought out and killed the

Minotaur in the Labyrinth of Crete. Fittingly, heroes cast in the Theseus mold are brave souls who take on a dangerous task. The audience must be encouraged to root for the hero, whose perseverance and appeal make him (or her) the audience's surrogate. The hero gains favor because this person (or team) maintains the moral high ground, which connects humankind to what is decent and good. The hero is bound by this moral imperative; if it is abandoned, the cause (and the story) may fail. (Ironically, the motion picture titled *Hero* was not successful because the main character was ambiguous about holding the moral high ground.) (1996, 25)

As we know, of the six archetypes Dortort suggests, the hero is used most often in movies and the quest of the hero is the one most often imitated.

Lucey too goes on to say:

The Buddy/Friendship archetype is based on the Damon and Pythias myth and always features two friends who take on the world *(Midnight Cowboy, Of Mice and Men)*. The archetype may deal with comedy teams whose variations include "I can do it better than you" *(The Odd Couple)* or working together against a common enemy *(Romancing the Stone)*. The buddies may display a love–hate relationship as they battle enemies *(Outrageous Fortune)*, or they may become dependent on each other *(White Men Can't Jump)*. (1996, 25)

As we'll see, the Buddy/Friendship archetype can also be associated with the *mentor* relationship that Campbell talks about.

According to Lucey, it's not so much the impossible quest as it is the quest itself and the quest itself can be applied to all these other archetypes in one way or another.

The Impossible Quest archetype relates to characters who undertake a noble adventure search, or journey, rather than setting forth to defeat a villain. Such stories, based on the Icarus and Daedalus myth, can be humorous, innocent, tragic and uplifting at the same time *(The Right Stuff, Boys on the Side, Searching for Bobby Fischer)*. Stories using the Impossible Quest archetype often set up an objective (help E.T. escape, cure the disease, find the treasure) and then show how the characters either achieve the goal or fail in their quest. However done, quest stories use the main characters to demonstrate the nobility and resilience of the human spirit. (1996, 26)

"The king must die"—the Breaking-Away archetype—in Lucey's discussion of "Dortort," deals with parent and child conflicts, or situations where the old order must yield to the new.

Breaking-away stories take many forms, as when parents wish to hold on to their children *(The Heiress)* or a husband–wife rivalry requires the child's presence *(Irreconcilable Differences)*. The archetype is shown clearly in the film *Breaking Away,* in which a boy not only turns from his family's blue-collar traditions by enrolling in college, but breaks away from his childhood friends to begin another life. Another example is sexual rivalries between parents and the child's loved one *(Class)*. The Breaking-Away archetype can be laden with blood memories *(The Trip to Bountiful)*, Oedipal conflicts *(Psycho)*, sibling rivalries *(The Fabulous Baker Boys)*, and abandonment fears *(Paper Moon)*. (1996, 26–27)

The Breaking-Away archetype ties into two major life moments—separation of children from parents and individuation, a need to achieve a sense of self. Separation and individuation are among humankind's most powerful drives; when a person is denied this kind of growth, mental illness, loneliness, anger, impotence, drug abuse, gang-related activities, and other problems may result. Often it takes years for a person to form his or her own identity, which is why the struggle to individuate is the basis for many fine scripts *(Five Easy Pieces, What's Love Got to Do With It?, Postcards from the Edge)* (excerpted from Lucey 1996, 27). But as we'll see, breaking away is a constant in any character transformation since the character must make a transition from one way of being to another.

Lucey says Dortort's descriptions of the first four archetypes—Hero, Buddy/Friendship, Impossible Quest, Breaking-Away—come from

> Hellenistic traditions that envisioned humans in an uneasy relationship with watchful gods who were alert for signs of human pride or arrogance (called *hubris*). The Medea archetype came from a later tradition that is based on the idea of womanly power. Legend has it that Medea helped Jason secure the Golden Fleece, became his wife, and bore him two sons. When Jason spurned her for another woman, Medea invoked her sorcery, murdered her rival, and punished Jason by destroying what he loved most: his sons. The Medea archetype thus veers away from earlier patriarchal archetypes by presenting an independent woman who is unfettered by male dominance. Regina in *The Little Foxes* connects to the Medea archetype, as do the powerful women in *The Last Seduction, Disclosure, Fatal Attraction, The African Queen, The Joy Luck Club,* and other films. (1996, 27)

The Faust archetype is based on a sixteenth-century German legend (Johann Faust) who reputedly gave his soul to the devil for gifts of magic, beauty, and youth. [This] archetype usually deals with the extremes to which people will go to get what they want. There is a devilish quality to many Faustian stories because the wealth, knowledge, and power that flow to the main character often spring from corrupt sources. On this basis, Faust stories often struggle with moral values. Some writers follow a more redemptive view of Faust, seeing him as a symbol of humanity's heroic striving for knowledge and power. This approach was pursued by Goethe in his epic poem, *Faust,* which [has] inspired operas, plays, and other literary works. (1996, 27–28)

Although general, Dortort's examples are very useful; however, when we apply them to what Campbell has written, the direction you may want to go in terms of character development becomes much clearer, as you'll discover in the next section.

Character: Development and the Quest

Joseph Campbell's text, *The Hero with a Thousand Faces*, was first published in 1949. What this book does is draw extensively from world mythologies and on the works of psychology to approach the quest of the hero–protagonist as an exercise in personal enlightenment and self-fulfillment. I mentioned earlier that the notion of *the quest* is likened to a kind of rite of passage as well, and most all film characters go through some kind of *rite of passage*. The cultural anthropologist Arnold van Gennep, in a book titled *Rites of Passage*, wrote:

> The life of an individual in any society is a series of passages from one age to another and from one occupation to another. Wherever there are fine distinctions among age or occupational groups, progression from one group to the next is accompanied by special acts, like those which make up apprenticeship in our trades. Among semi-civilized peoples such acts are enveloped in ceremonies, since to the semi-civilized mind no act is entirely free of the sacred. In such societies every change in a person's life involves actions and reactions between sacred and profane actions and reactions to be regulated and guarded so that society as a whole will suffer no discomfort or injury. Transitions from group to group and

from one social situation to the next are looked on as implicit in the very fact of existence, so that a man's life comes to be made up of a succession of stages with similar ends and beginnings: birth, social puberty, marriage, fatherhood, advancement to a higher class, occupational specialization, and death. For every one of these events there are ceremonies whose essential purpose is to enable the individual to pass from one defined position to another which is equally well defined. Since the goal is the same, it follows of necessity that the ways of attaining it should be at least analogous, if not identical in detail (since in any case the individual involved has been modified by passing through several stages and traversing several boundaries). (1961, xxx)

So too do we see rites of passage apparent in screenplays. One of the clearest examples of a rite of passage on both a personal as well as an anthropological level is in *Apocalypse Now* in which the Martin Sheen character goes on a quest and through a rite of passage. It certainly isn't coincidental that two of the most influential twentieth-century books written on cultural anthropology and the quest—Jessie Weston's *From Ritual to Romance* and George Frazer's *The Golden Bough*—are included in one of the more dramatic shots of the film.

Not only do those books testify to the notion of how character and quest are inextricably connected, but they are fundamentally grounded in the notion of storytelling itself. The *Apocalypse Now* title is clear on that subject in that the word *apocalypse* is Greek for "revelation" and, political statements and homages to Joseph Conrad notwithstanding, it is Sheen's *revelation* that really is the focus of the story. That kind of revelation can also be seen in films as structurally dissimilar as *Run Lola Run* and *Matchstick*

Men. What we'll be looking at in this section is the relationship between character development and the quest and its influence on the writing of screenplays.

In the opening of his text, Campbell writes:

> The standard path of the mythological adventure of the hero is a magnification of the formula represented in the rites of passage: separation, initiation, return— which might be named the nuclear unit of the mono- myth. A hero ventures forth from the world of common day into a region of supernatural wonder: fab- ulous forces are there encountered and a decisive vic- tory is won. The hero comes back from this mysterious adventure with the power to bestow boons on his fellow man. (1972, 30)

This journey transcends time and culture. Whether the hero–protagonist is from west or east, north or south, "the adventure of the hero normally follows the pattern of the nuclear unit above described: a separation from the world, a penetration to some source of power, and a life-enhancing return" (Campbell 1972, 35). Examples of this sort abound: Jesus, Buddha, Moses, Prometheus; choose your hero.

"Typically the hero of the fairy tale achieves a domestic microcosmic triumph, and the hero–protagonist of a myth [has] a world–historical macrocosmic triumph" (Campbell 1972, 37–38). In other words, in the myth, the hero–protagonist returns with something that will not only regenerate the imme- diate or extended community as a whole, but returns with something *for* the hero–protagonist as well. What the hero–pro- tagonist returns with may not necessarily be something tangible (e.g., a trophy), but in fact something intangible (e.g., love). The macrocosmic scheme of this quest is simplified into three stages:

- Departure or separation
- Initiation
- Return

As I said earlier, within each of these major sections come subsections, seventeen to be exact, though not all of them are used in cinematic plots of the hero–protagonist because the majority of the stories deal with notions of personal spirituality, which may not exactly fit within a cinematic storyline.

The usefulness of Campbell's work in terms of plot structure *cannot* be underestimated since it simplifies and unifies the act of storytelling and, to a great extent, offers a kind of road map for character development.

In many commercial films, and all "quest" films (e.g., *The Name of the Rose, Indiana Jones, Romancing the Stone, The Fisher King*), the hero–protagonist inevitably experiences a number of obstacles that are integrated into the three acts of an Aristotelian play. These three Aristotelian acts are complemented by the following three segments that Campbell alludes to in the rite of passage.

ACT I
The Aristotelian "Setup" is the equivalent of Campbell's "Separation"

ACT II
The Aristotelian "Development" is the equivalent of Campbell's "Initiation"

ACT III
The Aristotelian "Resolution" is the equivalent of Campbell's "Return"

To clarify these acts, we then incorporate specific components into Campbell's scheme, namely the ones in the next chart:

ACT I

THE PLOT SETUP/THE
HERO–PROTAGONIST'S DEPARTURE (Separation)

1. Introduces the hero–protagonist within a recognizable environment
2. Establishes a framework for a problem or conflict for the hero–protagonist to undertake
3. Presents the objective of the hero–protagonist
4. Presents incidents that will propel the story forward to that point where the hero–protagonist . . .
5. Commits himself or herself to endure the hardships that accompany attaining the objective

ACT II

THE PLOT DEVELOPMENT/THE
HERO–PROTAGONIST'S INITIATION

1. Introduces the hero–protagonist to an unrecognizable or "foreign" environment
2. Presents obstacles, conflicts, subplots to the hero–protagonist's attempts at obtaining the objective
3. Moves the dramatic potential forward to its inevitable conclusion

ACT III

THE PLOT RESOLUTION/THE
HERO–PROTAGONIST'S RETURN

1. The hero–protagonist's struggle between good and evil
2. The hero–protagonist's objective is met
3. A satisfactory conclusion for the hero–protagonist is reached

Now let's take a look at the entire scheme.

ACT I
THE SETUP/DEPARTURE/SEPARATION

1. Call to adventure
2. Refusal of the call or the reluctant hero–protagonist
3. Supernatural aid or enter the mentor
4. Crossing the first threshold
5. The belly of the whale

ACT II
THE DEVELOPMENT/INITIATION

6. The road of trials
7. Meeting with the goddess
8. Woman as temptress
9. Atonement with the father
10. Apotheosis or deification
11. The ultimate boon

ACT III
THE RESOLUTION/RETURN

12. Refusal of the Return
13. The magic flight
14. Rescue from without
15. Crossing the return threshold
16. Master of the two worlds
17. Freedom to live

Once again, the scheme is absolutely necessary in attempting to formulate some notion of character development since

film characters do not develop without method and direction. The creation of storyline is not an arbitrary response to reality but, rather, a precise and structured response to reality even though it may appear to be *meandering*. To that end, almost every good screenplay demands that the character undergo some kind of alteration and come to some kind of revelation about the nature of reality and his or her reason for being. It is to that end that we take our own journey, which is devoted to character development and conflict.

In Quest
of Character

1. "Do you Know the Way to San Jose?"
or, Call to Adventure

This stage, the first one in the separation phase, is the beginning of the hero–protagonist's journey. It often, but not always, begins with what Campbell recognizes as a *blunder*, or something that implies the merest *chance*, which reveals an unsuspected world to the hero–protagonist; he or she is drawn into a relationship with forces that are not entirely understood (1972, 51). It may not be a blunder at all, but "some passing phenomenon [that] catches the wandering eye and lures one away from the frequented paths of [humans]" (1972, 58). Whatever the case, the blunder, phenomenon, or chance "may amount to the opening of a destiny" (1972, 51) and in that notion of destiny lies the true beginning of the tale.

When we first meet Charlie Babbitt (Tom Cruise) in *Rain Man,* he is an arrogant, self-centered son of a bitch. By the end of the film, his character has been developed to the point that Charlie isn't an arrogant, self-centered son of a bitch but a loving, caretaking brother. We need to "ring up the curtain" for Charlie, but how is that done?

The *call to adventure* for Charlie Babbitt comes when he's informed by Lenny, one of his employees, that his father has died. What does that information do in terms of initiating a character's development? We've already been put on notice that Charlie is self-absorbed. Now we find out a bit more in terms of why Charlie may be the way he is by virtue of his reaction to his father's death. But the death of his father also initiates a point of departure for his character to develop. The call from Lenny is Charlie's call to adventure because it initiates a series of incidents, which when overcome lead to the transformation of Charlie's character.

What's curious about a film such as *Babette's Feast* is that Babette (Stephane Audran) appears in the opening of the film, disappears while the backstory is played out, then reappears at about the film's 40th-minute when we discover that she's come to Jutland, Denmark to escape the Revolution. One can look at that escape as the *chance* Campbell talks about since she's been written a letter of introduction to the sisters by Achille Papin, the opera singer who once visited the church some thirty years before.

Be that as it may, at the 42nd-minute of a 102-minute film Babette is asked the question: "Don't you miss France?" to which she answers that her only link to France is "a lottery ticket." That's a supremely interesting comment because precisely at the 47th-minute, a letter from France arrives indicating that she's won the lottery! For the next sixty minutes (or about 60 percent of the film), the story deals almost entirely with "the feast" proper; in other words, the organization, preparation, and execution of the feast.

Although this *chance* offering comes much later than in *Rain Man,* it is remarkably the same in that many of the same questlike conflicts do happen to Babette, but in a slightly different way. What we see in both films is that some phenomenon occurs that alters the established ways of being for the individual characters.

In *Midnight Cowboy,* the *chance* deals with something much less obvious than either a letter or a call. It's something we haven't really seen yet, but it is engrained in the mind of Joe Buck (Jon Voight) who's obsessed with New York, as witnessed at the opening of the film during which he sings "get along little doggie New York's your new home." What seems to be the chance or, in his case, the *blunder,* that motivates Joe to leave Texas for New York is his rather provincial thinking that since he's a "stud" in a small Texas town, he can be a stud anywhere. To him, New York offers significantly more opportunities to make money than he has in Texas because the women all "want it" and the men there now are all tutti-fruttis. So for him the motivating device is his naïveté. That kind of provincial innocence makes him a perfect target for those who are living the urban experience, and it also creates enormous obstacles and conflicts for him to overcome.

In yet another example, what's the *blunder* that positions Benjamin (Dustin Hoffman) to become Mrs. Robinson's (Anne Bancroft) tool in *The Graduate?* We see Mrs. Robinson seduce Benjamin but that's not the chance. The *chance* was that she was at the party in the first place and that she manipulated him, as follows:

1. Asks him to drive her home, and he does
2. Invites him into her house, and he goes in
3. Asks him to stay, and he agrees
4. Offers him a drink, and he accepts
5. Seduces him, and he thinks otherwise
6. Convinces him to see Elaine's portrait, and he follows

7. Asks him to unhook her blouse, and he consents
8. Asks him to retrieve her purse, and he complies
9. Orders him to put it in Elaine's bedroom, and he obeys

All of these orders eventually led to the famous nude scene in which Mrs. Robinson propositions Benjamin. Hers was not a simple game of coincidence, but a contrived game of chance since at any time in Mrs. Robinson's scheme, Benjamin could have refused but didn't. So from Benjamin's bedroom to Elaine's bedroom, each game of chance shows us a bit more about Benjamin's character and, at the same time, prepares us for potential conflicts between Benjamin and Mrs. Robinson.

Other films contain numerous other examples of chance operating as the motivating feature in initiating character development. In *Brazil*, it's a fly that's accidentally crushed in a futuristic typewriter that changes the spelling of a name and alters the direction of the plot and creates a quest for Jonathon Pryce's character. In *Run Lola Run*, the *blunder* is Manni accidentally leaving a bag filled with money on the subway, and in *Rocky*, it's his chance selection to be Apollo's opponent.

What is truly remarkable about these blunders, or chances, or passing phenomena is that each one of them occurs within the first fifteen minutes of the film (except for *Babette's Feast*); in *Midnight Cowboy*, Joe Buck has quit his job at about the 3rd-minute and he's off to New York at about the 5th-minute.

Regardless of when or where the blunder or chance occurs, the *call to adventure* initiates what is the onset of a character transformation that the hero–protagonist undertakes as a result of events (obstacles, predicaments, dilemmas, conflicts) throughout the course of the film, but that are clearly initiated in the first act. To Campbell, this *call to adventure* "signifies that destiny has summoned the hero–protagonist and transferred him from a place like home to a place unlike home" (1972, 58). In other words, the "accident" takes the character from a "known" environment to an "unknown" environment.

As Campbell suggests, the new place can be both a region of treasure and source of danger. The place can take on the appearance of a distant land (e.g., Colombia in *Romancing the Stone*, Jutland in *Babette's Feast*), a forest *(Labyrinth, Robin Hood)*, a secret island *(Dr Moreau)*, an underground kingdom *(Indiana Jones and the Temple of Doom)*, a new world *(The Matrix, The Wizard of Oz)*, a new city *(Midnight Cowboy, Home Alone 2)*, an enchanted castle *(Harry Potter)*, or even an assortment of seemingly unknown place(s) within a known place *(Thelma and Louise, The Fugitive, Rain Man)*.

For Babette, the movement is from the glamour of Paris to the provinces in Jutland; in Disney's *Santa Clause*, it's Tim Allen's character movement from the confines of the comfy Midwest to the North Pole. In *Good Will Hunting*, it's the Matt Damon character's movement from the comfortability of South Boston to the rigors of academe at MIT. In Disney's *Toy Story*, both Buzz and Woody are *separated* from the friendly confines of Andy's bedroom in the old house, end up being *initiated* next door in the delinquent Sid's bedroom, then escape and *return* to Andy's bedroom in a new house as the best of friends—an almost identical situation happens in Disney's *Shrek*.

Wherever it may be, it is a place not visited before, or if it were visited before, the circumstances are different now. If a character is going to move from a known comfortable place to an unknown one of anxiety, you first must establish the character in his or her ordinary environment. The reason for establishing the old environment is to create a *contrast* with the new environment and implicit in that contrast is the notion of *conflict*.

As I said, the move may be a physical shift *from* a place like home *to* someplace totally unlike home, as in *The Matrix;* or it may be an emotional or psychological shift *within* the vicinity of home, as in *Breaking Away* in which the main character, Dave Stoller (Dennis Christopher), goes from idolizing Italian bikers to despising them. In *The Fisher King,* Jack Lucas (Jeff Bridges) goes from being a wealthy, highly successful and arrogant radio jock to a humble and reclusive video clerk who must find redemption; in *Possession,* Gwyneth Paltrow's character goes from being an uptight professor who tends to wear her hair in a chignon to being a loving and sensuous woman who finally "lets her hair down"; and in *Elizabeth,* the character Cate Blanchett plays goes from being the bastard child of Henry VII to the Queen of England.

So we can see that implied in a call to adventure is the presentation of a problem, a challenge, or an objective that must be satisfied by the end of the film. The hero–protagonist can no longer remain untouched by living in the tranquility of the normal world. As Campbell says: "The familiar life horizon has been outgrown; the old concepts, ideals, and emotional patterns no longer fit; the time for the passing of a threshold is at hand" (1972, 51). To remain at home would mean no conflict and no conflict means no story. We'll see this most dramatically when we get to the *Good Will Hunting* case study.

Regardless of the type of plot (action adventure, mystery, romantic comedy) you may want to write, the *call to adventure* initiates the action of the story. Without it, there is no storyline. But also implied in the call to adventure is conflict and that's something we will address in terms of character development.

Exercise

Time to brainstorm. We've seen some examples of chance, blunder, or passing phenomenon that initiate a call to adventure, so now come up with your own. You need to deal with these individual categories in a more precise and definitive way by brainstorming. What you should do is actually build a character and a storyline together, beginning with the *call*. This exercise is devoted to determining what you think is a creative, imaginative call to adventure—something unique that actually "brings up the curtain" on the adventure awaiting your hero–protagonist.

2. "Can't Go, I'm Busy" or, Refusal of the Call

Whatever the case may be, the call to adventure involves a change of direction, a change of purpose, and implicit in any change is the potential for conflict. To that end, then, the hero–protagonist may not want to deal with conflict since conflict is not comfortable.

In other words, at this point, the hero–protagonist may resist. After all, he or she doesn't know what's going to happen "out there" beyond the safety of the normal environment. In mythology and folktales, the story often goes no further than this; but if that were the case for screenplays, we'd be writing a short and not a feature. There may be a hesitation on the hero–protagonist's part, a momentary decision to stay where things are most comfortable. At this stage, something may pro-hibit the hero–protagonist from making a move, of initiating the change, and/or of attempting to break from the comfort of the common world. For the story to be told in earnest, however, refusal of the *call* is unacceptable.

In *Braveheart,* we first see William Wallace as a child who has witnessed the murder of his parents. He leaves with his uncle and isn't seen again for about another thirty minutes as much of the historical backstory is played out. When Wallace returns, he's no longer a child, but a man and is smitten with a young woman whom he wants to court.

It's clear that Wallace has fallen in love and is content to live peacefully on his land. However, the woman's father denies Wallace the opportunity of courting his daughter unless he takes a passive position against the English, which would inevitably mean continued subjugation by them. In order to have her, her father tells Wallace that he must be true to his word and not fight and he doesn't. On the other hand, the Scottish guerillas want him to join the fight as much as his father did. What even-tually causes him to *alter* direction is the murder of the woman, now his wife. At that point, all bets are off. Wallace was reluc-tant to act, seemingly content living the status quo; it's only after losing what he loves the most that Wallace takes action. By virtue of taking action, his character is altered.

How does that work in *The Graduate?* The *chance* of Mrs. Robinson appearing in the nude has, apparently, scared Benjamin enough that the last thought on his mind is taking her up on her offer. But summer vacations are long and boring, par-ents are often difficult to live with, and continual thoughts about the future hang like an albatross around his neck. So what does Benjamin do? He calls Mrs. Robinson, but then one sees that he has severe reservations about what he's done. These reser-vations continue in subsequent scenes leading up to their first meeting and the scene in which he chooses not to have sex with her; however, angered by her suggestion that he's a virgin, Benjamin changes his mind. At that point, there's no turning back. We've seen that when he has certain moral misgivings about what he's done, Mrs. Robinson isn't very happy, but once he's phoned her there can be no refusal of the call.

One of the best examples of this kind of hero reluctance is in *Rocky* when he believes that he's been chosen to be Apollo's sparring partner. However, when boxing promoter Jurgens informs him that he hasn't been chosen to be Apollo's sparring partner but his "challenger" for the heavyweight championship of the world, Rocky's anxiety level increases and he initially refuses. Not only is it clear through what Rocky says, but also through his nervous gestures that he has major doubts about whether he should fight. After all, this is an opportunity to fight the world champion—someone he idolizes. Since everyone thinks Rocky's a bum, and even he has reservations and calls himself a "ham and egger," why would he want to put himself in a position to be both soundly beaten and publicly humiliated?

But, something does drive these characters to seek *change*. There is something that motivates the hero–protagonists to take action, seize the opportunity, and, by so doing, alter the direction of their lives. According to Campbell, there is a "rejection of the offered terms of life, as a result of which some power of transformation carries the problem to a plane of new magnitudes, where it is suddenly and finally resolved" (1972, 65). In other words, by rejecting the everyday life and embarking on something new, two things present themselves:

1. The implied acceptance that potential problems (conflicts) may arise
2. The implied precondition that the new journey will be resolved in some fashion

So, whatever the case may be, we see some variation of the resistant hero–protagonist who, for whatever reason, was seemingly reluctant to make a change, but who nonetheless must change.

Exercise

You've established a call to adventure. Now, let's take what you've come up with and fabricate a reluctant hero–protagonist. What might that reluctance look like given what you already have? How might that reluctance advance character development? Try to think of reasons why the hero would not want to change. What are his or her reservations? What keeps the hero–protagonist engaged in staying within the normal environment and not ready to explore an unfamiliar place?

3. "Help, I Need Somebody" or, Enter the Mentor

But if a hero–protagonist is somewhat reluctant to take the next step, what's the best way to help him or her have a change of mind? Perhaps the hero–protagonist needs some kind of *assistance* and to that extent, "For those who have not refused the call," Campbell writes, "the first encounter of the hero–protagonist's journey is with a protective figure (often a little old crone or old man) who provides the adventurer with amulets against the dragon forces he is about to pass" (1972, 69). This particular figure represents the "benign, protecting power of destiny" (71).

"The higher mythologies develop the role in the great figure of the guide, the teacher, the ferryman, the conductor of souls to the afterworld" (72). So where does this figure enter in a film?

Often someone will teach and/or assist the hero–protagonist in accomplishing *something,* which may not appear entirely positive at the outset, but it may have positive value. For example in *The Graduate,* unlikely as it may seem, Mrs. Robinson is really Benjamin's *mentor.* He learns a great deal from her: she incites him to anger, causes him to confront authority, and challenges him to be responsible for his actions, even though these things are not explicitly stated.

In Waldo Salt's brilliant script, *Midnight Cowboy,* Joe Buck arrives in New York with the clothes and attitude to be a hustler. After several failures at picking women up, he finally succeeds, but in the afterglow asks her for money. Of course, she's outraged and the scene ends not with Joe getting paid for his studly services but with Joe paying her. Welcome to New York. Joe's out of his league and obviously in need of someone who "knows the ropes." Enter Ratso Rizzo who becomes Buck's urban tutor and enables Joe to survive in the asphalt jungle of New York. At some point during the story, there is a shift in the mentoring process—a kind of mutual mentoring that goes on; by the end of the film, it's Joe who becomes Rizzo's caretaker and in effect that shows how his character has arced from someone totally involved with himself to someone who can care for a person totally unlike himself.

Again in *Rocky,* after he's been selected to fight the champ, Mickey (Burgess Meredith), the gym owner and the one who kicked Rocky out of his locker, comes for a visit. We know the two of them have had a long and rather contentious relationship and it all comes to a head in the scene in which Mickey essentially pleads with Rocky to let him manage him and share his half-century of boxing experience with him. At first, Rocky is indifferent to Mickey, then that changes when Rocky vents a decade of repressed anger at Mickey's apparent indifference to him. But after the catharsis, the conclusion of the scene has Rocky making amends with Mickey because it's clear to him that not hiring Mickey would undermine his chances of "going the distance."

Although we'll spend a great deal of time discussing *Good Will Hunting*, what we see at the outset of the film is that Will is not your normal young adult. Also we discover that Will has had a load of legal problems and needs someone to bail him out. At first, it would appear that Lambeau (Stellan Skarsgård), the scholar, will be his mentor, but that's not the case. It's only when we meet the therapist, Sean (Robin Williams), who in his own way reprises the part of Berger in *Ordinary People,* that we realize who will assist Will in getting through the emotional and psychological problems he has.

Finally, in *The Matrix*, Neo (Keanu Reeves) seems to be the chosen one to receive the instruction of the underworld. But, who is capable of helping him? Who can possibly teach him? Who else but Morpheus (Laurence Fishburne) who has the knowledge, the skill, and the wisdom to teach the Reeves character the things he has to know about the matrix.

Whatever the case may be, the mentor's primary function is to *assist* the hero–protagonist in addressing the anxieties of the unknown and assisting in his or her transformation. By the same token, the mentor's role is limited. Eventually, the hero–protagonist must distance himself or herself from the mentor and go it alone. Rocky climbs into the ring with Apollo; Conrad must come to terms with the person who needs the most forgiveness; Benjamin needs to go beyond "the graduate." So, the mentor assists the hero–protagonist in a journey.

Exercise

Now we have rung up the curtain by initiating a call to adventure for the hero and incorporated a reason why he or she might be reluctant to do something out of the ordinary. But the hero–protagonist has made a decision to forge ahead regardless of the circumstances, regardless of the possible consequences. So what kind of mentor might she or he have at this point? What kind of character will the mentor be? What kind of role will the mentor play? What will the mentor do to assist the hero–protagonist in effecting change? Think in detail about what exactly this character can do to assist the hero–protagonist.

4. "To Boldly Go Where No One Has Gone Before" or, Crossing the First Threshold

With the fact that the hero–protagonist cannot stay within the boundaries of the normal, everyday world and experience the change that needs to be experienced, she or he must commit to the quest, and by committing to the quest, the character crosses the *first threshold* into an unexplored world. We already know that the hero–protagonist can't stay "home" but must commit to this quest to enter into a new world.

In *Romancing the Stone*, Joan Wilder (Kathleen Turner) has received a mysterious package, but what really incites her to action is the desperate call from her sister who's been kidnapped in Colombia. At that point, she must make a decision either to stay in New York and do nothing or to go to Colombia to help out her sister.

What we see is that she's completely inadequate for the task of traveling and that's been validated by her editor who says she gets sick riding an escalator; yet, she chooses to journey to Colombia and to deal with all the attendant problems associated with travel and a new culture, not to mention new and unknown dangers. Regardless of what potential disasters lay ahead, there's no turning back, and even though Joan knows she may be out there on her own, she's willing to take the risk.

In *Ordinary People*, Conrad (Timothy Hutton) has been consumed with nightmares about the night his brother drowned in a boating accident and even has attempted suicide because of it. The *threshold* for him is not only making the call to see Berger (Judd Hirsch), the psychiatrist, but in making the appointment.

Conrad finally gets the courage to visit the psychiatrist and even though the first appointment is not the most auspicious, once he has crossed over into the realm of the "new" he cannot cross back. In other words, he has chosen to move from the world he knows best to an unknown world though it's laden with anxieties. In effect, the decision to move will alter his character; to what degree, we don't know at that point, but his character will eventually change from a state of anxiety and apprehension to a state of self-realization.

For Rocky, when is the decision made? At what point is there a crossover from the normal, everyday world to the unknown world? Arguably, it is the moment when he begins to train. He was offered the choice to fight the champ; by accepting the offer to fight, Rocky tacitly commits to train. The moment he wakes up at 4 A.M., drinks a half dozen raw eggs, and begins to jog he's crossed the *threshold*—the hero–protagonist agrees to confront the possible consequences of a change in direction. There are *crossovers* between one stage and another.

As Aristotle suggested, the most important thing is the *structuring* of the incidents, and we've already established that the Aristotelian acts can be regarded as representing a beginning, middle, and end. It is at this point that the hero–protagonist makes a decision that will become unchangeable and lead him or her to the inevitable conclusion established at the outset.

In other words, a decision that's been made eventually will unify the ending with the beginning, or as Aristotle said: "link the beginning to the end with inevitable certainty." Any decision to move forward clearly ends the hero–protagonist's one way of being and creates a new way of being since the inevitable outcome of acting will invariably affect his or her character. So, in effect, crossing of the first threshold is also the *movement* from the beginning to the middle, or from Act I to Act II or from the setup of the incidents to the development of the incidents already set up.

Exercise

Now our character is well on his or her journey, has refused to live the status quo, and has acquired a mentor. What, then, is the character's initial turning point that will move him or her on the way? What incident and/or events will unequivocally change the direction of the story, and by virtue of what happens, unequivocally change the direction of the character?

With all of the preceding exercises accomplished, what exactly do you have? The foundation for Act I!

5. "Light, More Light!" or, The Belly of the Whale

In cinematic stories, this stage is really an extension of stage four since it gives renewed emphasis "to the lesson that the passage of the threshold is a form of self-annihilation" (Campbell 1972, 91). This stage means that by accepting the challenge presented to him or her, the hero–protagonist has agreed to "kill" whomever he or she was prior to the acceptance and has agreed to accept what might happen. In a way it's a process of being "born again."

Essentially, the crossing of the first threshold concludes the first act. In other words, stages 1 through 4 plus 5 comprise Act I of the play. Actually, we can see that Campbell's first five segments are equivalent to Aristotle's Act I because we've set up what's going to happen through the course of the story and to whom it's going to happen.

In effect, Crossing the First Threshold stage is tantamount to the transition between Acts I and II in which the hero–protagonist, who has now accepted the challenge, moves from the comfortable and mundane world—the world she or he knows well—into the foreign world of obstacles. Perhaps anxious, but no longer reluctant, the hero–protagonist must now learn whatever there is to learn about the outside world and, consequently, about herself or himself.

Essentially, this is the *boundary* (real or imagined) the hero–protagonist crosses, and this is the cinematic moment when the plot takes a different direction. Given the time parameters of feature films, this particular movement generally occurs at the end of the Act I. In short, it is the moment when the hero–protagonist decides to seek his or her destiny.

This section concludes the Separation phase, so an act has been completed.

6. "Take Two Aspirin and See Me in the Morning" or, The Road of Trials

This is the stage where the real work starts because in one's quest to become a hero–protagonist, to be initiated as a hero–protagonist, a number of obstacles will present themselves. Having crossed the threshold, Campbell writes that "the hero–protagonist must survive a succession of trials" (1972, 97). Even though the hero–protagonist has been assisted by a mentor, he or she must continue the journey primarily on his or her own. The point here is that the hero–protagonist will encounter all sorts of challenges (physical, psychological, emotional) that will test the fabric of his or her being.

To a great extent, this is the stage that will take the most time because it's here that numerous obstacles become apparent; the obstacles must be overcome to create a more whole individual. This is where the greatest character alteration (development) takes place because each obstacle forces the hero–protagonist to adapt.

In *Ordinary People*, Conrad has now committed himself to "getting better." But what obstacles are there to that goal? What things *must* he endure to get better? It's not only the psychological grappling that Conrad must deal with, but also social and domestic issues. The obstacles along his path must be overcome and overcoming them will alter Conrad's character. He must deal with his trying not to be in control throughout his therapy sessions, with his mother's emotional distance, with the newly found anxieties he has over a love interest, with his classmates.

34

Likewise, in *Rocky*, the obstacles are twofold: the psychological and the physical. By overcoming the physical obstacles, he will be in a better position to overcome the psychological obstacles. As Rocky increases his physical strength, there is a parallel increase in his psychological strength. During that process, he has to pursue a regimen of training that he's never pursued before. So, after he's accepted the challenge and acquired a mentor, Rocky now attempts to achieve what he has long thought was unachievable, especially because everyone has told him he was a bum. Rocky must overcome the image that others have of him, must deal with Adrian's (*sic*) brother Paulie, with Adrian herself, with Gazzo's driver, and with his newly gained celebrity. All these obstacles need to be overcome if he's to reach the goal he's set for himself.

In *The Graduate*, Benjamin and Elaine have been separated by virtue of the story Mrs. Robinson told her about her relationship with Benjamin. Feeling as if the one person in his life he can genuinely love has been taken from him, Benjamin assumes responsibility for his life and takes on the obstacles that have beset him in order to retrieve that love. The following are only a few of the obstacles and frustrated attempts that Benjamin must overcome to win Elaine back, but they clearly give us a look at what Benjamin must deal with to alter his character from what he was at the film's outset: Mrs. Robinson's lies, Mr. Robinson's disdain, Elaine's engagement, his lack of plans for the future. Benjamin must overcome all these obstacles so that his character develops from the rather naïve graduate he was at the beginning of the summer to someone else.

Finally, and, perhaps, most poignantly, in *Rain Man* Charlie (Tom Cruise) kidnaps his autistic brother, Raymond (Dustin Hoffman) and is holding him for ransom. But what Charlie doesn't know is that his brother's needs become the main obstacles that he must overcome for personal growth. What Raymond eats, when Raymond eats it, where his bed must be located, what kind of underwear he wears, his aversion to going out in the rain—all are demands that test the fabric of Charlie's character. Dealing with them forces him to move away from a preoccupation with his own self-interests to consider the needs of his brother.

The preceding are only a few of the obstacles Charlie has to overcome; however, not only has he learned to attend to his brother's needs, but, at a critical time in the film, he learns exactly who the Rain Man is and exactly what happened to him. This particular *midpoint epiphany* is an essential turning point in Charlie's transformation. After this realization, he makes amends with his girlfriend Suzann and "turns a new leaf."

Trials may present physical obstacles as well. For example, "the hero–protagonist may come to a dangerous place, sometimes deep underground, where the object of the quest is hidden" (1998, 24); it may be the antagonist's hideaway. When the hero–protagonist enters that space he or she is now within the phase of the Initiation per se. A fearful place is revealed in *Indiana Jones and the Temple of Doom* and in *Jurassic Park*. In practically any James Bond film, the physical obstacle is at the headquarters of the villain (e.g., *Dr. No, Goldfinger, Never Say Never Again*).

It is important to know how the hero–protagonist functions under physical, psychological, and/or emotional stress and how that stress will have a bearing on the character's arc. As Campbell writes: "The original departure into the land of trials represented only the beginning of the long and really perilous path of initiatory conquests and moments of illumination. Dragons have now to be slain and surprising barriers passed— again, again, and again" (1972, 108). So it's not one trial that has to be overcome by the hero–protagonist but a multitude of trials.

Exercise

Given what we've come up with so far, let's create some serious obstacles for the hero–protagonist and see if they can, in fact, elicit other obstacles. What's critical here is to create obstacles that *can* be overcome even though there may be new ones ahead. You need to focus on creating resolvable dilemmas regardless of their apparent complexity. As each new obstacle is presented, the hero–protagonist must overcome the obstacle and by virtue of overcoming it alter his or her character.

7. *"You Can Always Get What You Want" or, Meeting with the Goddess*

Probably a better way of stating this section's title would be "attaining the goddess" since "the ultimate adventure," says Campbell, is "when all the barriers and ogres have been overcome, is commonly represented as a mystical marriage of the triumphant hero–protagonist-soul with the Queen Goddess of the World" (1972, 109). Campbell suggests that woman represents the totality of what can be known (1972, 116) and that the goddess herself undergoes a series of metamorphoses, though ultimately, she is the hero–protagonist's guide to the attainment of the sensual and the sublime.

One might be able to synthesize this particular stage as "boy finally gets girl" or vice versa. He becomes the king of her created world. This relationship, which may or may not be obvious at the outset of the story (e.g., in *The Graduate*, Mrs. Robinson introduces Benjamin and us to Elaine via her portrait), is usually set up in the first act of the film; however, this particular situation is often seen in romantic comedies in which the female or male protagonist, after overcoming all the obstacles—the road of trials—presented to her or him, realizes the dream of ideal romance.

For example, in *4 Weddings & a Funeral,* we know that Carrie (Andie McDowell) and Charlie (Hugh Grant) have met at the first wedding. Even though they don't get off to the most auspicious of starts, they do end up in bed together before she has to leave for the United States. Subsequently, she gets married, then divorced; we meet them again at his wedding at which time he refuses to marry the woman he's engaged to because he realizes that she's not the woman he loves, but that the McDowell character is. So here Andie McDowell is the "goddess" and the bungling Hugh Grant is the hero–protagonist who, after surviving his panoply of trials, gets what he wanted all along.

Not coincidentally, in *Green Card,* Bronte (Andie McDowell again), a New York City horticulturist, needs to get married to get the apartment she's always dreamed about. Georges (Gérard Depardieu), a randy and somewhat gauche Frenchman, needs a green card to stay in the United States. Their marriage is clearly one of convenience; however, when the INS starts to investigate them, they are forced to spend time together to prove that their marriage is legal.

Their "odd couple" lifestyles clash and he even says to her, "If you want me to be a beast, I can be a beast." There are numerous obstacles they both have to endure and overcome to get what they want though, in the process, they get what they didn't think they wanted—that is, each other. Although he has to leave the country (because he screwed up in the interview), she retains the apartment and they get married, if not in reality then in theory, with the promise that they will eventually get together.

Stranded in a Punxsutawney, Pennsylvania, snowstorm after covering a Groundhog Day ceremony for the fourth year in a row, weatherman Phil (Bill Murray) declines a date from his producer Rita (none other than Andie McDowell), choosing instead to go to bed. It's déjà vu time when the next morning Phil awakes to the same early morning broadcast that he heard the day before. He shrugs it off, leaves the hotel only to be greeted by the Groundhog Day ceremony. Why's it happening? Do they observe it twice? The following morning, it's déjà vu again, and the plot takes on a kind of comedic *Twilight Zone* twist—he's planted in a kind of time warp where he's forced to repeat the day over and over. The process of reliving the same day until he "gets it right" is Murray's *road of trials;* by finally getting it right, he's rewarded and gets the girl who just happens to be . . . Andie McDowell.

Now, just to show you that it's not always Andie McDowell that these guys get, let's try another example. The *Notting Hill* film begins with loser William Thacker (Hugh Grant) working in a bookstore when the door opens and in walks Anna Scott (Julia Roberts), movie superstar. What ensues is an impossible love affair between them that includes obstacles such as the media invasion of one's privacy, William's reluctance to engage in an affair with a star, and dealing with the asinine antics of his mentally challenged roommate. But after overcoming all the obstacles in his path, she gives up her career to become a full-time mom and Hugh has won his goddess.

One may think that these kinds of films are all acted in by Hugh Grant, Julia Roberts, and Andie McDowell and are written by Richard Curtis, but there are others too, so let's see if this works with another film.

Although we know Joan Wilder in *Romancing the Stone* is an award-winning romance novelist, she spends most of her romantic evenings with a cat named Romeo. We also know that the mysterious package she receives turns out to be what she needs to free her kidnapped sister, so Joan flies to Colombia. However, she takes the wrong bus and ends up deserted and distraught in the jungle. Enter Jack Colton (Michael Douglas) and with him, she overcomes a panoply of miseries including mudslides, drug lords, treasure hunters, and so on.

We know the kind of obstacles that Joan had to endure in order to save her sister and on and on, and just when she thought she was going to achieve true love, Jack disappears. Ah, but we know she couldn't get out of the story without finally achieving the love of her life and she does; in the end, Colton reappears in New York with a yacht christened *Angelina* (after the character that we met at the beginning of the film) and the two presumably take the yacht to other marvelous adventures.

These are only a handful of films in which the hero attains his goddess or, in fewer cases, the heroine attains her god by virtue of passing the road of trials. We also see this stage in other films such as *Crocodile Dundee* or *Sleepless in Seattle* or *You've Got Mail* or any one of a number of romantic or adventure comedies (usually starring Meg Ryan). The romantic setup in the first act is developed in the second act and pays off in the third act with the film finishing or almost finishing with a final kiss.

If you'll recall in *Rain Man*, it is only after Charlie Babbitt has revelations about who Raymond really is that he calls Suzann (his girlfriend) who forgives him and subsequently meets him in Las Vegas. So this meeting with the goddess is the final test of the talent of the hero–protagonist to win the "boon of love" (Campbell 1972, 118). After going through and triumphing at all the trials and tribulations presented to the hero–protagonist, she or he then achieves the love that has been pursued throughout the course of the story.

Exercise

How then does one incorporate the boon of love into the story? What's the final achievement going to be? Where is it going to be? How will it impact the character's development? This aspect is set up early in the first act with the introduction of the love interest, but to attain the love interest, the hero–protagonist must triumph on the road of trials. What, then, are those comedic circumstances that will enable the hero to win the love of his or her life?

8. "Naughty Girls Are Not Nice" or, Woman as Temptress

This stage is also a bit problematic in terms of defining, in simple terms, what is going on with the hero–protagonist, but in this case, he must "surpass the temptations of her call, and soar" above it (Campbell 1972, 122). Obviously, there is the temptation of the flesh involved and "wom[en] above all, become the symbol no longer of victory but of defeat" (123). The stage is included within the Initiation phase because it may be yet one more obstacle the hero–protagonist must overcome to secure "hero-hood." But there may be others.

Certainly women like this are often found in films since the *femme fatale* is not a new idea. In *Fatal Attraction, Mortal Enemies,* and others, there appears to be one woman (the *goddess*) who is often set against another woman (the *temptress*) in which the genuine love of the one tends to offset the evil intents of the other resulting in some kind of victory for the hero–protagonist. One could look at the Elaine–Mrs. Robinson dichotomy, for instance.

We can see that this setup is in practically any James Bond film; I've included just one here. In *Never Say Never Again*, Bond has been in semi-retirement, but is called back into duty to deal with SPECTRE's latest Hitlerian scheme to control the world. Maximilian Largo (Klaus Maria Brandauer) has somehow stolen two cruise missiles armed with nuclear warheads, and Blofeld (Max von Sydow), the Saddam Hussein of SPECTRE, has vowed to detonate them if an impossible ransom isn't paid. As with all Bond adventures, there are at least two main female protagonists who take the forms of temptress and goddess. Let's summarize both of them.

We meet Fatima Blush (Barbara Carrera) early on in the film, but she's the femme fatale who threatens to kill Bond by blowing up his genitals; however, Bond counters and shoots her with a fountain pen cum bomb, which once again proves the "pen is mightier than the sword." Set against Fatima is Domino Petachi (Kim Basinger) (not coincidentally, a *dark* Carrera versus a *light* Basinger) whom Bond gets as a kind of recompense for saving humankind by getting rid of the bomb. Carrera is the temptress and Basinger is the goddess and, as in the previous case, Bond gets the goddess after suffering the road of trials. But, of course, it would appear that regardless of the major actors in question (Connery or Moore or Brosnan), Bond always gets his man and has his way with his woman.

Exercise

What kind of goddess and temptress can we envision who would work well in this situation? You've already created a goddess, but what can you come up with for a temptress? Once again, it's important to come up with a character who will play in contrast to the goddess you've created.

9. "Father Knows Best" or, Atonement with the Father

This stage deals primarily with the psychological manifestations in father–son relationships though, by extension, one can use father surrogates if fathers won't do. If there is no father figure for the hero–protagonist, or if the father figure is truly an ancillary one, then a mentor can act as a father surrogate.

Just as one example, in *Rocky*, Rocky alludes to the possibility that his father may not be alive. That is, when he talks about his father it's in the past tense; never is there any indication that his father is alive. We've seen that Rocky chooses Mickey to be his mentor, but Mickey is also portrayed as a father surrogate. There is a kind of atonement early on between the two of them and clearly by the time Rocky fights Apollo the two have reconciled all their differences, but that's not always the case.

In *Men of Honor*, Carl Brashear (Cuba Gooding Jr.) finally gets accepted into the Navy's prestigious Dive School program. His training officer, Billy Sunday (Robert DeNiro), is, as one would expect, a "hard-ass son of a bitch" who taunts and humiliates Brashear, presuming that such behavior will eventually make Carl quit. However, that's not the case and, over the course of the film, he comes to terms with Sunday.

In *An Officer and a Gentleman*, Zack Mayo (Richard Gere) has nothing and it appears he's going nowhere until he enrolls in the Navy's Officer Candidate School to become a pilot. Like Brashear, Zack has his own Billy Sunday in his "hard-ass son of a bitch" drill Sergeant Foley (Louis Gossett Jr.) who makes Mayo's life a living hell, even though Mayo refuses to quit. What we eventually see is that after layer upon layer of conflict between them, the Gere and Gossett characters finally fight each other and it is only after the physical confrontation, which Gossett wins by a swift kick to the genitals, that there is atonement between them.

The stage also often involves some "hope and assurance from the helpful female figure, by whose magic the hero–protagonist is protected through all the frightening experiences of the father's ego-shattering initiation" (Campbell 1972, 131). Certainly, the presence of Adrian (Talia Shire) has modified if not mollified Rocky's character in a significant way, as does Paula Pokrifki (Debra Winger) in *An Officer and a Gentleman* and Jo (Aunjanue Ellis) in *Men of Honor*. So one can see how there is a triangular situation among the hero–protagonist, the female or male supporting character, and a father or father surrogate in a character-driven script.

Certainly in a film like *Ordinary People*, Conrad's love interest Jeanine Pratt (Elizabeth McGovern) has had an impact on how he deals not only with his friends, but also with his father and mother. But it would appear that this particular stage is dependent on the dramatic potential of the storyline and that the storyline would have to include some aspect of father–son, or by extension father/surrogate–son, conflict for it to have any value in the script.

Exercise

Let's speculate on what kind of father/surrogate father relationship you can come up with as well and how that would work into character development. You can see that there is kind of a father/surrogate/mentor relationship here. You need to make a decision about what role the mentor is going to have; that is, if the mentor is also going to be an "adversary," then that has to be established early on. It is at this point that the hero–protagonist and the father/surrogate/mentor should come to some understanding of each other.

10. "God Only Knows" or, Apotheosis and Deification

This stage can also be a bit problematic in terms of using it as a marker in structuring a feature film since the stage itself is the *reaching of a divine state of being* for the hero–protagonist who has gone beyond the last terrors of ignorance. For Campbell, it represents "the release potential within us all . . . which anyone can attain—through hero-hood . . ." (1972, 151). One could look at it as some kind of revelatory stage within the Initiation phase, but I'm going to skip it and go on to the next stage, which is a bit clearer.

11. "Winner and Still Champion" or, The Ultimate Boon

As Campbell writes, ". . . the boon is simply a symbol of life energy stepped down to the requirements of a certain specific case" (1972, 188). The *boon* can be a request made with authority or the thing requested. As a thing requested, it can take the shape of something that will enable the hero–protagonist to *see* better. In effect, it does become a kind of *trophy* for having experienced the road of trials.

The Steve Tesich film, *Breaking Away,* is clearly a coming-of-age story with a minor ensemble cast of four characters not the least of which are Mike (Dennis Quaid) and Cyril (Daniel Stern). The main protagonist, Dave Stoller (Dennis Christopher) wants to be something he cannot—that is, an Italian cyclist. Hence, everything Dave does reflects that desire: singing Italian opera, speaking with an Italian accent, and so on.

Subsequent to a fight between Mike and some college students, the president of the university indicates that there has to be a kind of reconciliation between "town and gown" and invites a town team to participate in the Little 500 Bicycle race, which becomes the climax to the film. After an accident, Stoller tapes his injured feet to the pedals, rides to victory, and literally claims the *trophy*.

But trophies don't necessarily need to be inanimate objects. They can also be people. We witnessed a number of obstacles that Benjamin had to overcome in order to achieve the ultimate boon (i.e., Elaine). The one last obstacle is, arguably, the most difficult; only after Benjamin sprints to Elaine's wedding, seizes a huge metal cross, and locks Elaine's family and friends inside the church can he claim her as his trophy. What remains is a mystery to both of them and us, but at least they have each other.

Richard Gere does much the same thing in *An Officer and a Gentleman*. After Gere made amends with his father figure/mentor, Foley, he's graduated from the Navy's Officer school and only has one thing left . . . to retrieve his trophy by returning to where his love interest Paula (Debra Winger) works, picking her up is his arms, and walking out with her.

But the ultimate boon or trophy doesn't necessarily need to be a person either. It can also be money. Certainly, an argument can be made that the money Lola won at the gaming tables in *Run Lola Run* has become her trophy since, from her perspective, it saves her love interest, Manni, from certain death and keeps him for herself.

In *Rain Man*, Charlie Bobbitt's trophy is, quite simply, the understanding of what love means—nothing tangible at all—and that's best revealed in the last scene of the film.

Then too, in *The Matrix*, it is Neo's recognition that he is actually the "chosen one." Ideally, the hero–protagonist should have learned something from the experience that makes the person a more well-rounded human being. In that sense, the character *arc*, which we discussed before has been completed.

Trophy is the appropriate word because a trophy is anything that serves as a *token* or *evidence* of victory, valor, power, skill, and so on. But the trophy can be merely the symbolic representation of what the hero–protagonist has discovered about himself or herself. All of these things (both tangible and intangible) can be considered trophies and the attainment of such generally concludes the Initiation phase and leads to the last phase—the Return.

Exercise

What's the trophy going to be for the character you've created? What exactly are you going to have the hero–protagonist achieve? Will it be something tangible or an intangible? Will it be something that demonstrates that she or he is worthy of achieving it? This is really the "endgame" of the script since this is the point at which the hero–protagonist has attained whatever she or he set out to attain. For that reason, whatever is attained as the trophy needs to be something significant and redeemable.

12. "You Can't Always Get What You Want" or, Refusal of the Return

As Campbell writes, the return trip, "requires that the hero–protagonist shall now begin the labor of bringing wisdom, the Golden Fleece, or his sleeping princess back into the kingdom of humanity" (1972, 193). This stage begins the Return phase. Sometimes the responsibility is refused; however, in film that would tend to put a damper on the climax, so there can be no refusal of the return but there may be . . .

13. "Catch Me If You Can" or, The Magic Flight

What usually happens in this stage is that the "trophy has been attained against the opposition of its guardian, or if the hero–protagonist's wish to return to the world has been resented by the gods or demons, then the last stage of the mythological round becomes a lively, often comical, pursuit . . . complicated by marvels of magical obstruction and evasion" (Campbell 1972, 197). This stage is what can be called the *retreat from danger.*

For example, Indiana Jones retrieves the stone for the people of India, but he still has to return the stone to its proper guardians. Bond always seems to "come up with the girl" at the end of the film, only to be chased by the evil wrongdoers whom he thinks he's already finished off.

In a way, it's a kind of *backfire* element that one finds regardless of the type of script being written. Essentially, it is that point in the script where the hero–protagonist thinks he or she has accomplished all that needs to be accomplished, yet there remains one last obstacle to overcome.

In cases such as these, it is imperative that the hero–protagonist receive . . .

14. "Help, I Need Somebody!" or, Rescue from Without

"The hero–protagonist may have to be brought back from his supernatural adventure by *assistance from without,*" says Campbell. That is to say, "the world may have to come and get him" (1972, 207). As indicated earlier, this situation always seems to happen to Bond—he's gotten himself in too deeply and needs to be bailed out. This kind of scenario usually happens in films in which "the cavalry comes to the rescue" after the hero–protagonist has done something for the welfare of the community.

The Bond film *Never Say Never Again* is no different. With Bond and his partner Leiter (Bernie Casey) in trouble deep in the undersea bowels of Largo's hideaway, they are eventually rescued by reinforcements and that enables Bond to go after his main antagonist.

We also see this situation in films, such as *Last of the Mohicans,* in which the army comes to the rescue. This stage brings us to the final crisis, that being the supremely difficult threshold of *crossing* from the mystic realm *back* into the life of the everyday. Essentially, it is that moment when the hero–protagonist, at the ultimate moment of crisis, is assisted from outside, which finally leads us to . .

15. "Been There, Done That" or, Crossing the Return Threshold

As I've said, the hero–protagonist ventures out of the land she or he knew into the unknown land. Once there she or he "accomplishes the adventure . . . and the return is described as coming back out of that . . . zone" (Campbell 1972, 217). But the hero–protagonist must survive the "impact of the world" to complete the adventure. In other words, the hero–protagonist needs to readjust to the *reentry.*

Rocky, beaten and bloody, goes the distance, being "resurrected" (as the opening scene suggests) as a heavyweight contender, not a bum; Benjamin goes against all the odds (both mathematical and moral) and captures Elaine; Baskerville (Sean Connery), in *The Name of the Rose,* comes through the flames of hell and survives with manuscripts that he's saved; Charlie Babbitt finally loves; Conrad finally cries.

Unless a *trophy* is brought back from the initiation and *across the threshold,* the hero–protagonist has not been duly initiated, and therefore has learned nothing. If the hero–protagonist has learned nothing, then there's no story unless, of course, the learning of nothing, which is something, is what he or she has learned.

It would appear that this particular stage would conclude the *quest* of the hero–protagonist, and, to a great extent, it does because the storyline has been concluded. The *arc* of the hero–protagonist has been completed and problems have been resolved. With that said, there can be no other film better suited than the *The Wizard of Oz,* which concludes with Dorothy clicking her heels as she returns to Kansas with the discovery that she is loved and that "There's no place like home."

There are others, to be sure—Rocky's discovery that he can "go the distance" with the champ and that he's not a bum; Benjamin's discovery that being an adult means taking responsibility. The return that the hero–protagonist makes is truly the final act of self-discovery and must reflect the final maturation of the character arc.

Exercise

Now you've gone the distance, so what can you come up with that will satisfy as an ending? What, in fact, has the hero–protagonist of your tale learned? What, in effect, is going to be your final statement in terms of how the hero–protagonist has developed, what he or she has learned, what has been accomplished, and so on?

16. Master of the Two Worlds

17. Freedom to Live

These last two stages are generally disregarded in terms of structuring a screenplay for a standard feature. *Master of the two worlds* is that stage in which the hero–protagonist has somehow been transfigured and by suffering the road of trials has mastered the world she or he came from and now is better suited to be master of this new world. Presumably, the *freedom to live* allows the hero–protagonist to be "the champion of things [that are] becoming, not of things [that have been], since he [now] *is*" (Campbell 1972, 243).

In a curious way, though, these two stages could be looked at as preparatory stages for a sequel or sequels in that the hero–protagonist has learned something and that learning will, in some way, prepare him or her for other stages of life. One could make an argument that these two stages are a kind of preconditioning exercise for subsequent films since the ending of one film could lay the foundation for the next. With that kind of scheme, we could easily follow Rocky, for example, throughout the sequels to see if, in fact, this would work; but, as in the Bond films, there remains the "virtue of the repetitively constant" to enable the story to succeed and to that extent each script essentially repeats, with modifications, the original storyline and carries that character forward with the least amount of alteration.

If you've done all the exercises to this point, you should have a detailed and focused point of departure and point of destination for your character. In essence, what you should have is a treatment for your script, a kind of script template, on which you can now fashion a script in its productive form.

51

Summary of the Quest

So, the following is how we can schematize Campbell's quest of the hero–protagonist and, by extension, your hero–protagonist.

- Your hero–protagonist sets forth from his or her everyday life in which everything is as it should be; in other words, the normal environment. — *ordinary world*
- Someone or something suddenly presents your hero–protagonist with a way to change that everyday life into something completely different. — *call to adventure*
- Your hero–protagonist isn't sure about leaving "home" since this is the place or circumstance that he or she knows well, but does so albeit reluctantly. — *reluctant acceptance*
- On the way to achieving the goal, your hero–protagonist encounters someone who will help him or her in attaining whatever needs to be attained. — *mentor*
- Your hero–protagonist then has to overcome a laundry list (road) of trials and tribulations. — *obstacles, complications, subplots*
- When your hero–protagonist overcomes the ultimate obstacle, she or he earns a reward for achieving what she or he set out to achieve. — *trophy*
- The triumph may be represented as your hero–protagonist's sexual union with the goddess–mother *(marriage),* a son's recognition by the father *(atonement),* and the attainment of "hero-hood." — *champion*
- The final work is that of the Return. If the powers have blessed your hero–protagonist, he now returns with some help; if not, the evil forces come after him. — *escape*
- At the Return threshold, the powers must remain behind; your hero–protagonist reemerges with something gained. — *return, resurrection*

If you've followed this correctly, you should have a fairly clear outline of what needs to be done to flesh out the entire script. The next sections are additional exercises that are meant to help you develop character and conflict. These schemes will, in fact, help you to organize the flow of the script.

Clearly, what we've discovered throughout the Quest is that character is action. If you establish a clear quest for the character, then you can incorporate the kind of action necessary to reach the goal.

General Principles of Conflict

To this point, we've been talking about character and, at times, conflict and how the latter relates to the former. Now let's deal with this notion of a *dramatic conflict* in a more substantive manner. *Conflict* is a great word; it comes from the Latin *conflictus,* "a striking together, a contest," and *confligere,* "to strike together." So, the definition is something like a fight or battle, a contention, to clash—something that is antagonistic. *Antagonistic* comes from *ant*—against—and *agonistes*—actor. In other words, someone who is to *engage in conflict* with the *protagonist*.

Without a conflict between or among parties, there is no dramatic potential, and without dramatic potential, we have a work of little import. This notion of striking together is not new. According to Moore:

> Stanislavski said that because life is a continuous struggle, on stage as in life there are counteractions of other persons, facts, circumstances, events, opposing logic of actions. Conflicts and struggles create interesting collisions. A valuable dramatic work is always based on struggles between different persons. Spectators are carried away by the process of a struggle. A person is pushed to act, to express his [sic] own interests, when

these interests clash with the environment. *An actor must find the obstacles in the way of his [sic] character and try to overcome them.* [emphasis added] (1974, 76)

In screenwriting, the writer invents the obstacles that the actor must overcome. But how? We've been discussing, and at some length, the whole notion of the Quest in relation to the development of the hero–protagonist's character, but how does one then incorporate the notion of conflict?

We can begin by using Lawson's definition: "the essential character of drama is social conflict—persons against other persons, or individuals against groups, or groups against other groups, or individuals or groups against social or natural forces—in which the conscious will, exerted for the accomplishment of specific and understandable aims, is sufficiently strong to bring the conflict to a point of crisis" (1967, 168).

The *point of crisis* is also a goal. In large measure it is what the hero–protagonist seeks at the outset. But the goal which [the character] selects must be sufficiently realistic to enable the will to have some effect on reality. We, in the audience, must be able to understand the goal and the possibility of fulfillment. The kind of will exerted must spring from a consciousness of reality which corresponds to our own (Lawson 1967, 167). But however weak the will may be, it must be strong enough to sustain the conflict.

Dramatic potential cannot deal with characters who are weak-willed and unable to make decisions that have even temporary meaning, who adopt no conscious attitude toward events, or who make no effort to control their environment (Lawson 1967, 168). What results with these kinds of films is that the main characters do not develop or develop immaturely; because of that lack of development there also is no sufficient and plausible arc. The conflict, if there is one, is neutral in the sense that it does not contribute in any dramatic way to the overall development or growth of the character. We will see an excellent example of this later when we get to the film *Driven*.

What character can be the hero–protagonist? Clearly, any character who is "strapped" with conflicts to overcome—the more conflicts to overcome, the richer the character will be. Dumas, the Younger wrote that before every situation a dramatist creates, he should ask himself three questions: What should I do? What would other people do? What should be done? Each answer to these questions should encompass the notion of conflict.

If, at the outset, the hero–protagonist is not thrust into a dilemma, a confrontation, a situation that manifests as something "out of the ordinary," then your basis for dramatic potential is weak; if your basis for dramatic potential is weak, then your conflicts will be weak as well. What that results in is a hero–protagonist who is one-dimensional at best, a cardboard figure at worst.

The first 10 to 15 percent of a film, which translates to about 10 to 20 pages of script, is the most critical. What you do with those pages may well determine the success, artistically and commercially, of the entire production, regardless of length. We've seen, clearly, that certain elements must be incorporated immediately and that those elements must be integrated into the notion of conflict.

It should be evident that a motivation, emotional and/or intellectual, needs to be enacted by the hero–protagonist if we are to believe what we see and can see something to believe in. As Gessner tells us:

> The key is *enactment*. Visualization implies movements that are dramatic and cinematic and has been called the *IAC: Idea into action through character* [emphasis added]. In every shot, scene, and sequence there should

be an idea in motion focused on the character who dominates that image. He [sic] may be the protagonist or supporting character, but if the moment belongs to him—for whatever dramaturgical reason—his action as a character will largely determine the effectiveness of that moment. (1970, 102)

Gessner continues to state that the conflict that is depicted when an idea goes into action through a character's feelings or deeds is generally seen in connection with a choice. A hero–protagonist may have more than one target to shoot at. Gessner likes to use the triangle to reflect these interpersonal conflicts because, as a means of identifying and sorting out the characters, it lines up the teams before the game commences; it can organize conflict; it can aid in character development. As a device by itself, the triangle is not cinematic, nor does its existence automatically guarantee a cinematic application. The cinematic triangle, in other words, has sharper points. So how do these triangles work in scripts? Triangles reinterpret and redefine the original triangle by sharpening the conflict and compressing character interplay (Gessner 1970, 104).

Another characteristic of an effective triangle in cinema is the opportunity it provides for a *running* conflict. Let's, then, take the notion of conflict and divide it into two categories by using the following: *neutral,* or homeostatic, conflict—not really going anywhere in particular—and *ascendant,* or positive conflict—gradually increasing in tension and contributing to the hero–protagonist's development. Before we start using these two types of conflict, it would be a good time to interject that even though these aspects of conflict are discussed individually, they don't work that way. They work, like cinema itself, in a very synergistic—a very integrated—way. Thus, to discuss conflict without discussing how it coalesces with character would be a bit like teaching one to tango without a partner. So, let's go back to something discussed earlier, the *character arc.*

As stated previously, the character arc is that *range of action* a character makes from the point of departure, where she or he began, to the point of destination, where she or he ends up. In other words, the storyline must present a situation that will engage and force the character to change, thereby altering the circumstances of his or her character. As noted, nothing creates the need for change more dramatically than conflict.

The character arc also engages the *story arc,* those situations that parallel the character through the change and initiate the *question to be answered* (QBA)—what the storyline implicitly poses at the opening of the script that must be ultimately answered by the end of it. For example, *Rocky* presents that situation quite effectively because the QBA—*Will Rocky remain a bum?*—which was initiated at the outset, is answered by the end of the film: no. And what contributed to that change? Both internal and external conflicts.

In a film like *Amélie,* the character of Amélie Poulin is established early on as someone who's lost her mother, is somewhat distanced from her father, and doesn't really have someone to call "her own." Though she's excellent at matchmaking and "doing the right thing" for others, the QBA is: *Will Amélie find someone for herself?* In the end, the answer: yes. And what contributed to that change? Conflicts, both internal and external.

In *Run Lola Run,* we discover that Manni owes Ronnie some drug money that he unwittingly left on the subway. For fear of being killed by Ronnie, Manni is desperate to find a way to replace the money. So the main storyline begins with a kind of desperation on Manni's part. He's already at the bottom and there are only two choices: find the money and live or not find the money and die, which begs the QBA: *Will*

Manni find the money and live with Lola? In the end, the answer: yes. And what contributed to that change? Conflicts, both internal and external.

How about *Good Will Hunting?* What might be the QBA there?—*Will Will remain a bad boy?* And how about in *Driven?* Can we come up with a QBA that's really satisfied by the end of the film?—*Will Jimmy be a champion* and *Joe make a comeback?* In the film, the problem with the former is that Jimmy's already one of the best drivers on the circuit. The problem with the latter is that we already know what his job is supposed to be so there's no surprise because there's no conflict inherent in the QBA.

Neutral or Homestatic Conflict

Let's take a character who exhibits a neutral or homeostatic type of conflict. What would that look like? It would appear that the two are mutually exclusive. In other words, how can you expect a character to exhibit any kind of dramatic conflict if he either wants nothing or doesn't know what he wants? This type of conflict is homeostatic—not moving, not exerting force of any kind—in the sense that it doesn't attempt to go anywhere.

Characters who cannot make a decision vital to the integrity of the storyline or to their own characters exhibit *homeostatic* conflict. In other words, you cannot expect a rising conflict from a character who wants nothing or does not know what she wants (Egri 1972, 137). As I've written before, dialogue that does not inject conflict is wasted dialogue. Only conflict can generate more conflict, and the first conflict comes from a conscious will striving to achieve a goal that was determined by the premise (Egri 1972, 137). Even though we're not addressing dialogue directly, you can see how critical writing dialogue is in relation to creating and advancing both character and conflict.

At the outset, a script can have only one premise, but, in a way, each character has his or her own premise that clashes with the others; however, all of them must further the script's main premise. We've seen how that works with *Rocky*, but how might that work in another film, say *Driven*?

What we'll analyze in detail in *Driven*, especially in terms of conflict, is that there is no substantial change in the characters. There is a modicum of conflict, but it is neutral or homeostatic. Almost all of the characters remain at the same level throughout the film. The problem? Little contrast. The majority of these characters are exactly alike and none of them has any deep convictions, and without any deep convictions, there is no dramatic potential. Without a kind of attack and counterattack, there can be no rising dramatic action. Where do these characters start and where do they end?

To that end, if the hero–protagonist's point of departure is known, we also have to know his or her point of destination. Without knowing the point of departure, there is no way you can develop a good character. For example, if the characters demonstrate the points of departure, shown in column 1, you can anticipate their points of destination, shown in column 2.

Points of Departure	Points of Destination
Drug abuse	Freedom from drugs
Shyness	Self-esteem
Infidelity	Fidelity
Emotionlessness	Emotional
Procrastination	Takes responsible action
Delinquency	Nondelinquency

If you know your character has to move from one point to another, then you can develop her or him at a steady rate and every conflict you inject will contribute to steady change, moving that character to the point of destination. These movements have to be executed in the most orchestrated of ways. In other words, there must be a legitimate cause and effect to make the development of the character appear plausible.

Positive or Ascendant Conflict

We can look at *ascendant* conflict as the result of a clearly defined premise and well-orchestrated, three-dimensional characters who exhibit a definitive character arc. Returning to *Rocky* once again, we discover, in the course of 11 minutes or almost 10 percent of the film, a lot of things about Rocky's character and about the direction of the story.

In terms of *plot*, we know that the film will deal with some aspect of boxing, an action that is conflictual, and that it will probably involve a character and situational change from bad to better that is also conflictual. In terms of *character*, we know a number of things about Rocky: he's good, lifelike in dialogue and action, and Stallone's portrayal is believable and consistent. In terms of *thought*, we know, even in a nonverbal way, what kind of things Rocky thinks about—that is, what things are important to him: family, religion, friendship, love. In terms of *diction*, we know how the hero–protagonist speaks and what his language reflects sociologically since his accent situates him in a particular socioeconomic milieu. But most important, we witness a clearly defined point of departure which, if properly orchestrated, will present both internal and external ascendant conflicts that will increase the tension and move toward a point of destination that will satisfy the premise.

Gessner defines *drama* as the reaction of a character to crisis. Such a definition provokes questions such as: Who or what causes the crisis? How do the characters react to the crisis?

How did antagonist and protagonist become entangled in it? Who else is involved and why? What is at stake? What will happen if the crisis is not resolved? Such questions also develop the plot because the crisis usually connects to a task that the hero–protagonist must accomplish. When we create a problem, it should cause a life-shaping and/or life-threatening personal crisis for the main characters. Successful stories are dramatic because of the hero–protagonist's ordeal, or series of ordeals, fits in precisely with what we've talked about in terms of the road of trials and the road of trials, is something that upsets the *status quo*.

As we know, the *status quo* refers to whatever conditions and relationships are in place when the story begins. This perspective on a story can provide another tool for developing the plot. To use it, you need only to see the inciting incident as something that interrupts the status quo in a way that initiates a crisis. Often, interruption is caused by the arrival or departure of a character.

In many cases, the interruption of the status quo is clearly a kind of call to adventure that initiates certain events that are different from the usual. In *Good Will Hunting*, the status quo is disturbed when the problem to be solved is mysteriously resolved.

The preceding discussion only reinforces what Stanislavski has already addressed: As protagonist and antagonist battle, the conflict moves the story toward the climactic moment when hero or villain will triumph. From this perspective, dramatic conflict is the hero's *struggle* against another person, system, or force outside himself or herself.

Awareness of the varieties of dramatic conflict can help you to figure out how it can be created and dramatized. This awareness is also a major tool for determining what will happen in the story being developed and is a useful guide to the conflicts presented by Paul Lucey in his book, *Story Sense,* in which he categorizes them in the following manner:

- Hero-versus-villain conflict
- Hero-versus-nature conflict
- Hero-versus-the-system conflict
- Hero-versus-the-self conflict

These are good points of departure to think about in relation to conflict, but regardless of who or what he or she must battle, the conflict must, invariably, advance the hero–protagonist's character through change.

Now that we've discussed both character and conflict and their interrelationship, it's time to deal with specific issues of character and conflict; to that end, I use *Good Will Hunting, Driven,* and *Amélie* as case studies.

Case Studies

Good Will Hunting

What I explore here, in some depth, is an analysis of character development using three significantly different films: the American films, *Good Will Hunting* (1999, 125 minutes) and *Driven* (2001, 109 minutes), and the French film, *Amélie* (2001, 122 minutes). It is highly recommended that you *screen these films* before reading this section.

All of these films are presumably character-driven, yet what the latter American one lacks, the former doesn't. Coincidentally, these two films were allegedly written by actors, not writers, and both were written with the same actors in mind to play the leading roles. I use a lot of what we've been discussing in terms of the character's quest and conflict to these films to see if they apply and, if so, how well those things apply.

Presumably, the *Good Will Hunting* screenplay was written by both Matt Damon and Ben Affleck, though the credits don't say "Screenplay by" but "Written by," which is not the same thing. There has been a lot of controversy about the script. In the February 1998 issue of *Written By*, Damon said:

> We met with a lot of studios and they were basically saying, "This is what we'd want to do with it." And we went with the place that we thought was the smartest

place for that movie. And there was a lot of development. There was a lot of rewriting that went on once we went to Castle Rock, and when we went to Miramax. There were a lot of really good meetings—we met a lot of really good writers, from Terrence Malick to William Goldman to Ed Zwick. There were a lot of people who were friends of the court who came in and threw in their two cents for us, which was great. It was really helpful.

Add to that what Goldman himself wrote in *Which Lie Did I Tell:* "I think the reason the world was so anxious to believe Matt Damon and Ben Affleck didn't write their script is simple jealousy. They were young and cute and famous; kill the fuckers." He went on: "When I read it, and spent a day with the writers, all I said was this: Rob's [Reiner] dead right. Period. Total contribution, zero" (Goldman 2000, 333). It would appear the jury is no longer out.

Regardless of who allegedly wrote and/or doctored the script, what's clear about the film is that it neatly adheres to many of the basic principles we've been discussing in terms of the quest and does so in a very efficient manner. Let's see how the opening scenes work that way.

Opening Scenes

The storyline begins with Will being picked up by Chucky and his friends. It's apparent that Will lives in a very poor section of what we soon discover is South Boston. Almost immediately we get "the ordinary world" established, the introduction of the two most important characters in the film (Will, Chucky) and two somewhat important supporting characters are presented (his friends); all of this is done in seconds.

The scene then cuts to a classroom at MIT during which the professor, Lambeau (another main supporting character, Stellan Skarsgård), says that he's put an advanced phoria system problem on the main hallway's chalkboard hoping that someone in the class will prove it by the end of the semester. He enumerates those who have solved it, a list that includes Nobel laureates.

Cut to the next scene in which we discover that Will is a janitor at MIT. As Will mops the floor, he stops and notices the problem on the board and ponders it. So now we know his normal job and his normal routine.

Next is a bar scene with Will and Chucky during which Will decides to go home. This appears to be something uncharacteristic of him, but it advances his character because in the next scene Will is standing in front of the mirror thinking about, then solving, the problem. He returns to his job the next day and answers the nearly impossible question on the board. The scene that follows shows Will and Chucky playing baseball—a scene that continues to advance both their characters.

What's excellent about these scenes is that they waste no time telling what must be told. Barely into the first five minutes of the film, we know a lot about Will: where he lives, who his best friend is, what his job is, what kind of mind he has, what he does for recreation. The scenes all contribute to character development.

Soon, the theorem solution is revealed, but who did it? No one claims responsibility. Again out with the boys, Will first goes to a baseball game where we are introduced to a guy who, apparently, beat up Will when he was in kindergarten; afterward, we see Will and friends get some burgers. These scenes are also crosscut with scenes at MIT, so what we have are parallel scenes of Will and his marginal friends with the privileged academics of MIT. In other words, we see the world in which Will operates and the *unknown world,* or the world of which he's merely an observer.

Suddenly, they pass a group of guys and one of them is the guy who beat up Will so many years before. They stop the car and a fist fight ensues with Will finally getting revenge for his childhood beatings. We do, however, have to suspend our disbelief to believe that after all those years Will never before had an opportunity to beat the hell out of the guy, but we do. Then the cops show up.

Back to MIT where Lambeau sees that no student has taken responsibility for the solution, so he sets up a new problem and a new challenge.

Back to police headquarters with Will stating that his arraignment is the following week.

Back to MIT where Lambeau sees Will at the chalkboard; Lambeau tells him to quit writing graffiti and Will takes off, but not before telling him to "fuck off." When Lambeau turns to the chalkboard, he sees that Will was answering the new problem.

What is clearly being presented here is, as in *Breaking Away*, a "town-versus-gown" kind of situation. That is, a relationship between marginal, blue-collar people who work hard for a living and live in South Boston versus privileged MIT and Harvard students. That juxtaposition is a conflict in and of itself and is one that breeds additional conflict, which is what we see in the next clip.

Bar Near Harvard

Once again we see Will out with the boys, but rather than frequent their "home" bar, they decide to go to the Harvard area. This scene is a terrific one in which Chucky (Ben Affleck) tries to pick up one of the young women, Skyler (Minnie Driver), and gets hassled by a Harvard student who recognizes that Chucky's not a student at all but merely a working-class kid in the "wrong" neighborhood. At that point, Will intervenes.

What we discover here about Will is something in addition to his ability to work with numbers. It's one thing to have this innate ability to deal with figures in a unique way; it's something else to be able to read whatever one reads and "integrate" that knowledge. Whereas the Harvard student has merely memorized passages and repeated them, Will has integrated what he's learned. That's a difference between knowledge and nominalism. By doing what he does, Will does three things in the scene:

1. He reverses the intellectual humiliation that the Harvard student wanted to inflict on Chucky.
2. He intimidates the student so that he backs out of a potential fight.
3. He impresses Skyler who sees something different about Will.

The scene ends with Skyler giving Will her phone number and the sequence is finished when Will flashes Skyler's telephone number to the Harvard student.

Of course, we have to suspend our disbelief once again in order to believe that Will's genius had never been recognized before. Clearly, he went to high school and, clearly, there had to have been a math teacher there who recognized his talents; however, we buy into his character because he's convincing and because we want to believe that he's somehow been overlooked if not ignored.

Lambeau then goes on a mission to find out who Will is. He finds out, then finds him at the arraignment at which time we learn a number of other things about Will.

Will in Court, Will and Skyler, Lambeau and Will

It's revealed that he's been accused of assault, auto theft, mayhem, and more and that he's been in foster homes and was abused. But in every case Will's defended himself and every case has been overturned; however, this time is different because Will hit a cop, a violation that will send him to jail. Just how Lambeau found out where Will would be is another mystery, but we buy it just the same. We also see a continuation of character development in what the judge says about Will. In a *layering* of his past we discover his previous crimes and his victimization by abandonment and abuse. All of these layers contribute to rounding out his character.

From jail, Will calls Skyler and asks if she's got some legal connections which leads us to the next scene with Lambeau. This is an interesting scene because it really does several things:

1. It is Will's *call to adventure* (a chance offering).
2. It shows him as a *reluctant hero* (studying math, he'll consider; therapy, he won't).
3. It offers him a potential *mentor* (Lambeau).

If Will agrees to what the court has offered, he's free to leave, but Will isn't stupid. He obviously takes Lambeau's offer in order to get out of jail, but that doesn't mean he's going to cooperate.

What ensues are two scenes in which Will essentially bullshits his way through the therapy sessions; however, his actions are not irrelevant. He's therapy-resistant for a number of reasons not the least of which is the fact he doesn't want to reveal any part of himself to anyone else. He knows that and we know that. So it's yet one more layer to creating an entire picture of who Will is as a character.

Frustrated beyond all reason, Lambeau tries to think of someone who might help Will and that's when the therapist, Sean (Robin Williams), is introduced. While Lambeau tries to convince Sean to take Will on, we see Will, once again, hanging out with the boys. These cuts between Will's *mentors* and Will's *home boys* are significant because we see those situations in which he is most comfortable and how his character alters when he's with his friends and when he's with others. This part of his character is never more obvious than when Will meets Sean for the first time.

Sean and Will Introduction

By this point, it's clear that Sean, not Lambeau, is going to be Will's mentor and, presumably, he is going to put him on the "right path." What's interesting about this relationship is that Will is going to help put Sean on the right path as well; this mentoring relationship is a bit different in that regard. Yes, there are actually two mentors: Lambeau mentors Will (or at least tries to) on a practical and intellectual level; Sean mentors Will on an emotional one. What we see is that Will, the intellectual, dismisses Lambeau's help; but Will, the emotional cripple, embraces Sean's help. On the former level, Will needs no help; on the latter level, he needs quite a bit of help. But Will can't do that alone. He can't get in touch with his emotional side with only Sean's help; Will desperately needs Skyler.

Will and Skyler: The Backstory

In the on-a-date scene, the two characters reveal more backstory and we get to see how they "mesh." Skyler's strength, beauty, and emotional resilience mesh with Will's need for those things in a woman. He knows he's intellectually superior to her, so that's not what he needs from her. He needs some kind of emotional understanding, but, at the same time, he fears any kind of emotional commitment. This scene is followed by Will's second session with Sean during which Sean does all the talking. Essentially he calls Will's bluff by confronting the main issue—Will protects his emotions through his intellect—and then challenges him by saying: "It's your move." End of session.

In several quick scenes, we see Will get picked up by Chucky, call Skyler and hang up without speaking, and go out with the boys. Once again, the scenes tend to focus on character: he bullshits his friends by saying he got a wrong number, but in fact Will's having second thoughts about Skyler. A relationship with her would involve commitment and commitment means revealing more of oneself, of allowing a veritable stranger into the domain of his protective environment.

In his third session with Sean, an hour goes by without anything being said. Lambeau appears and seems worried about that. Their fourth session appears to be heading in the same direction but then Will finally talks.

Sean and Will, Session 5 and Session 6: Bosox

The true breakthrough between them occurs when Sean talks about the fact that his wife used to fart in her sleep. That exchange humanizes Sean in Will's eyes because they can both laugh about it. But it also allows Sean to use that admission as a point of departure to illustrate intimacy between people who love each other, so the notions of love and intimacy become the foci of the scene. It's not coincidental, then, that the subsequent scene has Will and Skyler in bed together and that the scenes that follow show the two of them talking more and more about each other's past.

In their sixth session, Sean and Will discuss the time Sean met his wife and that it was the same day as the sixth game of the 1975 World Series; Sean gave away his tickets to see the Red Sox play to be with his newly discovered sweetheart. Clearly, the scene focuses on the choices that a person has to make in life. For Sean, the choice to forego an important Bosox game to be with the woman he loved was no choice at all. Sean's decision not to go to the game offers Will an additional insight into himself. So, it's no coincidence that the next scene has Will and Skyler in bed together at which point she says she won't sleep with him again until she gets to meet his friends. There's a little hesitation on Will's part because the moment he lets her meet his friends, he lets her into his world. To let her into his world is to share an intimacy that Will's reluctant to do.

Skyler, Will, and Friends at the Tavern

Finally out with the boys, Skyler tells a joke that's even dirtier than the jokes Will's friends tell, but the scene is integral for a number of reasons:

1. It shows that she can be "one of the boys."
2. It shows how fond Will is becoming of Skyler.
3. It prepares us for a conflictual situation since she wants to meet his family, a family he doesn't have and which he's lied about.

Lambeau, Sean, Chucky

The following scene has Lambeau and Sean discussing Will's future. There is a conflict between the two of them that apparently stems from their history together and one can see how each of them has his own perspective on what would be best for Will. In the end, however, Lambeau tells Sean that he already set up an interview for Will and in the following scene we see that it's not Will who shows up for the interview, but Chucky. Chucky turns the situation into a comedic moment by pretending to be Will and fleecing the interviewers of $70 in cash. The fact that Will sends Chucky only validates who his real mentor is: Sean. In fact, he's constantly denying Lambeau's assistance and sending Chucky to the interview only confirms his lack of respect for Lambeau and Lambeau's world.

Will and Skyler: The Truth

The next two scenes are very revealing in terms of character development because they are very climactic. Skyler needs to study organic chemistry, and Will says he'll help. She refuses, but Will can't take no for an answer and returns to her room with answers to her problems. They go out and then return to her room.

In a reenactment of the cliché "you only hurt the one you love," Skyler asks Will to leave with her for California. He hesitates. An argument ensues during which Will tells Skyler the truth; then he tells her he doesn't love her and promptly walks out. Torn between his love for her and revealing the truth about his life, he reveals the truth. Will can't deal with the consequences, so he chooses to abandon love and walks home alone.

Next, we see Will in Lambeau's office and in a confrontational scene he basically tells Lambeau that being with him is a "waste of time" since everything he does in math is easy and not challenging. The subtext to that scene is that there's no risk involved in math; however, he's also not able to take a risk at true intimacy either as evidenced by the previous scene. Will walks out on Lambeau and returns, naturally, to be with the boys. What's unique about this situation is that Will is caught in between the normal and the unknown worlds.

In previous quests we've seen the hero leave the ordinary world and enter the unknown world. In this case, Will doesn't truly leave but, in a way, straddles both worlds refusing to accept either one. What follows is a job interview, which Will does attend and which becomes a very clever segue.

NSA Interview, Sean Segue

Not only does the scene play as an answer to the interviewer's question, but as an answer to one of Sean's questions: What do you really want to do? By the end of the scene, Will actually answers Sean's question while simultaneously answering the interviewer's.

Will equivocates and that equivocation forces Sean to say "playtime is over" and he eventually kicks Will out of his office. This scene is highly reminiscent of the *Ordinary People* scene in which Berger says almost the same thing to Conrad. Whether it was "borrowed" from that film or not is irrelevant; the issue is that Sean can now do and say those things to Will because Will is "captured." That is, Sean has more control of Will's confidence at this point and knows more about his psychological matrix than anyone else. Sean won't stand for Will's equivocation and that's why he kicks him out.

The scene that follows is revealing as well. It's the last scene between Skyler and Will, and it works quite effectively in relation to Will's character.

Will and Skyler: The Kiss-off

Skyler is about to leave for California. Skyler, who is emotionally more healthy than Will, has no trouble saying the words *I love you* over the phone. Will's answer is, "Take care." But there's a subtext to that comment. For most women, it is easy to say "I love you" if, in fact, one is in love. For men, especially men who live by their intellect, it is not easy to say that; instead, they look for a euphemism like "take care." One shouldn't be led to believe that Will doesn't care or is not in love. To the contrary, for him to have gone to the airport would have been totally out of character and that's what makes the scene so effective. While she's on her way to California, he's sitting by the Charles River pondering what to do next. Will could not leave Boston because Skyler wanted him to;

that would have gone against his character. Will has to make the decision on his own and come to terms with "what he wants to do." This was a very clever scene and one that had to be there, since it prepares us for the *permission* scene that comes later.

The following scene has Will working construction juxtaposed with another scene with Lambeau stating that Will hasn't shown up for a meeting with Sean and, to him, that is problematic since it jeopardizes his probation. What follows this is the permission scene in which Chucky essentially gives Will permission to be the person he's supposed to be.

Will and Chucky

During the scene, Chucky basically tells Will he's wasting his life in Boston, and the key line is Chucky's admission that nothing would make him smile more than if he knocked at Will's door and Will didn't answer. That line in and of itself permits Will to leave. The permission could not have come from Lambeau or Sean or any of his other friends. It had to come from Chucky.

Another confrontation between Lambeau and Sean over Will's future follows, but that scene is not as important as the seventh session between Sean and Will.

Sean and Will: Penultimate Meetings

This scene is also highly reminiscent of the final Conrad–Berger scene in *Ordinary People* in which Berger, sensing Conrad is at his most vulnerable, knows that he must get him to emote now or never. Sean senses the same thing—it's now or never. Unless Will's emotional barrier can be broken, unless Conrad can overcome his guilt about being alive, just as Will must overcome his feelings of guilt about being abused, there can be no recovery and no chance to move on with his life.

Chucky has given Will permission to leave and Sean has given Will permission to cry. With those two things in hand, we find

Will on the subway alone, pondering his future. The next day he goes in for an interview, presumably arranged by Lambeau, and then we see him return to Sean's office for the eighth and last time.

In the final session, Will discovers that Sean is leaving too. Will has traveled the *road of trials,* has crossed the *threshold,* and has *returned* a different person. Sean's role as mentor has been completed and there's nothing left for him to accomplish. Just as Will is now a free man, so is Sean. They hug and Will leaves.

So it is not serendipitous that the boys give Will a car for his twenty-first birthday since the car is their way of saying: "We've given you permission to leave, now we've given you the means." What follows is a last meeting between Sean and Lambeau during which they resolve their own differences.

The Wrapup

The final sequence of scenes is worth noting because they neatly tie up everything. There are crosscuts of Sean packing up his apartment, Will showing up and leaving Sean a note, Chucky and the boys at Will's house. Chucky knocks on Will's door, but Will doesn't answer. Sean retrieves the note that indicates Will is making a choice between the job offer and the woman he loves, which is both an allusion to the choice Sean talked about earlier and the same words he used. Chucky realizes Will isn't there and he gives us the smile he alluded to earlier.

The final shot is of Will on the highway heading west, which links us to the beginning. Just as Chucky drives up to pick up Will at the beginning, Will is driving to pick up Skyler at the end. In terms of Will's character arc, it's clear. In the beginning, Will's arrogant, cocky, protective of his emotions. In the end, he's responsible, emotional, in love.

This brings us to the notion of conflict. There are two types of conflict in dramatic scripts, with attendant degrees of each—positive conflict and neutral conflict. *Neutral conflict* produces no positive character development for the hero–protagonist. In other words, neutral conflict between and among characters has no relative significance in determining the growth of him or her nor is it important in resolving the plot. On the other hand, *positive conflict* is conflict that may eventually lead to resolution and contribute to character growth. What's instrumental about positive conflict is that it really carries the character through the storyline. Likewise, the same thing holds for Will Hunting; if we construct a conflict chart for him, we get the following.

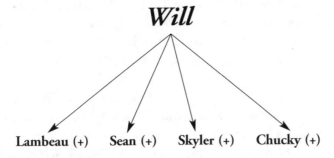

The Good Will Hunting Character/Conflict Chart

Will

Lambeau (+) Sean (+) Skyler (+) Chucky (+)

Will is in positive conflict with Lambeau. Even though Lambeau tries to befriend Will, Will is constantly in conflict with him; in the end, Lambeau's influence is negative as witnessed by the scene in which Will walks out on Lambeau as the latter is on his knees. Will is also in conflict with himself. At the outset it seems as if it will be a negative, unresolvable conflict, but it turns out to be a positive conflict with himself in that he changes.

Lambeau is in positive conflict with Sean because the two of them have to disagree with each other in terms of Will's best interest.

Sean is in positive conflict with Will because Sean will be instrumental in altering Will's arc, just as Raymond alters Charlie Babbitt's arc and Berger alters Conrad's arc.

Chucky is in positive conflict with Will even though the two might have disagreements. After all, they're dear friends and that kind of conflict is understandable among friends.

Skyler is in positive conflict with Will even when he refuses to see her off at the airport, and she has no conflict with any of Will's friends.

Will Hunting

Is Will Hunting much different than Benjamin Braddock? Will too changes dramatically from the beginning to the end of the film. His character arc is clear: He begins as a troubled, cocky, emotionless young man and becomes a responsible young adult. He goes from not taking chances to taking a lot of chances, from not loving to loving. He's a reluctant hero. For better or worse, Will finds a mentor in Sean, undertakes and overcomes considerable trials, and finally wins the love of his life. The positive conflict he has with Skyler has to be there for the story to succeed and for him to overcome what he needs to overcome.

We could do the same thing with Conrad in *Ordinary People* because the same elements are there. The positive conflicts with psychiatrist Berger, with his father and his mother, with his girlfriend; they all contribute to the character's arc and clearly development in characterization is shown.

So what can we make of positive/negative conflict? Certainly you need both and we'll see that, even in *Driven*, there are both types of conflict. So what's the difference? What matters is the dramatic potential of the positive and negative conflicts since it's the conflict between and among the characters that drives the story to its final conclusion. If the conflicts are not very well drawn and if the character is weak then what you'll end up with is a flat, lifeless story.

Benjamin Braddock

Obviously, there are degrees of positive conflict—some are stronger and more important than others. In *The Graduate*, the conflicts Ben has with Elaine are as important and as character-enhancing as those with Mrs. Robinson. But what we need to keep in mind is the impact that conflict has on developing the hero–protagonist. If the conflict has beneficial results in terms of transforming her or his arc, regardless of who elicits the conflict, the conflict is positive. If the conflict has no effect on the hero–protagonist's development, it is neutral at best and negative at worst.

Another example in *The Graduate* is when Mrs. Robinson is an antagonist, but elicits positive conflict, and Elaine, who is not an antagonist, elicits positive conflict as well. In the end, Benjamin's relationship with Mrs. Robinson is insignificant in terms of how the story ends. Though negative conflict is needed in order for Benjamin to arc, it's positive conflict that connects the storyline. To that end, what is significant is his relationship with Elaine; if we charted Benjamin's conflict, it would look like the following.

The Graduate Character/Conflict Chart

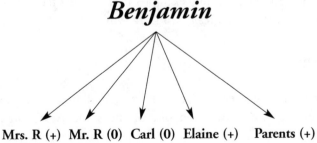

Benjamin

Mrs. R (+)   Mr. R (0)   Carl (0)   Elaine (+)   Parents (+)

Benjamin is in positive conflict with Mrs. Robinson, Elaine, and his parents.

Mrs. Robinson is in neutral conflict with her husband (they divorce) as well as with Elaine.

Mr. Robinson is marginally instrumental in the storyline.

Carl (Elaine's fiancé) is in neutral conflict with Benjamin and, from the ending, with Elaine as well.

Mr. and Mrs. Braddock appear to be in positive conflict with Benjamin, but their characters are phased out as the film progresses.

Elaine is in positive conflict with Benjamin and in neutral conflict with everyone else.

Let's take a look at the film in terms of Benjamin's characterization.

Ben changes dramatically from the beginning to the end of *The Graduate.* His character arc is clear: He begins as a passive, self-effacing, young graduate and becomes an adult. He goes from being well-dressed to messy, from not taking chances to taking a lot of chances, from not loving to loving. He's a reluctant hero; for better or worse, Benjamin finds a mentor in Mrs. Robinson, undertakes and overcomes considerable trials, and finally wins the love of his life. The positive conflict he has with Elaine has to be there for the story to succeed and for him to overcome what he needs to overcome.

So with the preceding examples in mind, let's take a look at a project that doesn't really work: *Driven.*

Driven

I was teaching a seminar at the Film in studium de Universität Hamburg, Germany when one of the students said to me: "We've seen a lot of examples of good character development, why not show us an example of some bad character development." I thought that was an excellent point. But I kept asking myself: "Where can I find an example of *bad* character development?" I was so used to trying to find *good* character development, I hadn't given much thought to finding something bad. Suddenly it came to me, like the light out of the east. I said, "We've got a perfect circle. Why didn't I think of it before . . . Stallone."

The reason I say Stallone is because the character arc of his writing career is a curious one indeed in that we know his first writing endeavor, *Rocky*, won the following awards in 1976:

- Oscar nomination for Best Original Script
- Writers Guild of America Award for Best Original Script
- Golden Globe nomination for Best Original Script
- Golden Globe and Academy Award nomination for Best Actor
- Golden Globe and Oscar for Best Picture

That's an incredible start for a budding screenwriter, and we'd have to think that superb things were in store for a writer with such immense talents at such a young age. Twenty-five years later, however, we find that Stallone's film, *Driven*, won the following awards in 2001:

- Golden Raspberry Award for Worst Script
- Worst Supporting Actor
- Worst Screen Couple—the Stallone and Burt Reynolds characters

It would appear that something's gone terribly wrong when that happens, and one could easily question how such a thing could happen. I've spent a lot of time discussing and presenting workshop ideas about character development. Previous parts of this book have shown how characters can and must change by using excerpts from the Tarot to Joseph Campbell.

But what happened here? What really differentiates *Rocky* from *Driven* or *Rain Man* from *Driven* or *Good Will Hunting* from *Driven* or practically every other film mentioned before from *Driven*?

To a great extent, the good films we've been discussing are good in terms of character development for the very reason they develop. The word *develop* comes from the Old French—"to unfold or unwrap"—and that's exactly what happens with well-written characters . . . that is, they unfold. If you look at a character as something rolled up, a long sheet of paper for example, then through the process of unrolling the paper, of unraveling the paper, you can see the entire sheet from beginning to end. A bit is revealed, then a bit more, like layers being peeled away. In the same way, the character at the end of the sheet shouldn't be the same as the character at the beginning of the sheet. So, all of the things we've been discussing seem to be pertinent to the whole notion of character development.

Enough has been said about *Good Will Hunting* for you to get a good idea of how Will develops from the beginning of the film to the end. We see how the individual conflicts, both positive and neutral, contribute to that character's development. But how does Joe Tanto (Sylvester Stallone) develop from the beginning of *Driven* to the end? Does he develop in the same way? Does he develop in a different way? Let's explore that now.

Opening Scenes

In a series of rapid cuts and dissolves, the film opens with scenes from races—from Long Beach, California to a race in Australia. By the time we get to Australia, we discover that the competition between the presumed antagonist Beau Brandenberg (Til Schweiger) and Jimmy Blye (Kip Pardue), the presumed hero, has yielded the following results:

Long Beach—No results recorded

Portland—Brandenberg comes in first; no mention of Jimmy's finish

Miami—Jimmy second

Mexico—Jimmy second; announcers claim "he's a natural"

Brazil—Jimmy first, Brandenberg second

Unknown race—Jimmy first (actual venue can't be discerned)

The Australian race is supposed to be Race 11 of the season even though we've only seen and/or heard about seven of them. What we do know from the Australian race is that Brandenberg has lost three in a row, not necessarily all of them to Jimmy, and seems to be "in trouble." But because he's a veteran driver, no one's thinking about finding a mentor for him. Shortly before the race, we also see Brandenberg breaking up with his fiancée, Sophia (Estella Warren), and the latter walks off after removing what appears to be an engagement ring. We really have to suspend our disbelief to believe that on the morning of a major Formula One race one of the best drivers in the world would tell his girlfriend to "piss off," but let's buy it. By the end of the race, Brandenberg has won, Jimmy has lost, and, apparently, the turmoil of splitting up hasn't bothered Brandenberg at all.

The next race takes place in Chicago and once again Brandenberg wins because Jimmy spins out on the final lap. It's at that time that Carl (Burt Reynolds), the car's owner, says they need Joe Tanto (Sly Stallone). But before we bring in the help, let's review the results again:

Long Beach—no results recorded

Portland—Brandenberg first; no mention of Jimmy

Miami—Jimmy second

Mexico—Jimmy second; he's called "a natural"

Brazil—Jimmy first, Brandenberg second

Unknown race—Jimmy first

Australia—Brandenberg first

Chicago—Brandenberg first, Jimmy second

By the end of these races, Brandenberg and Jimmy are *tied* for the lead for the world championship. That fact alone would beg the question: "Why send for Joe Tanto if Blye's doing so well?" It's not as if he's been losing all the races and is out of contention, in which case no one would need Joe Tanto. In terms of plot development, it doesn't make much sense. It would make more sense if Jimmy began on top and fell disastrously due to some emotional or psychological failing (an Aristotelian race tragedy), but in this scenario he comes out of nowhere as a rookie and is tied for first. But let's believe that he really needs help and so Carl seeks out Joe Tanto.

Carl Calls Joe

Joe is at home on his farm somewhere in the South when Carl calls and basically tells him he's driving for him. Joe isn't reluctant. It's not as if he hesitates about returning to the racing circuit again. So after a number of years out of racing (we don't know how many), Joe replaces Memo (Cristián de la Fuente) as Jimmy's racing partner; the scene shows him arriving in Toronto for the next big race.

We also meet Jimmy's brother, DeMille (Robert Sean Leonard), who is also Jimmy's manager and seems to be focused on one thing only: making money. Now in Toronto, Sophia has apparently traveled from Australia to Canada to follow the guy she broke up with. That fact begs the question: Why? Why follow your ex-fiancé halfway around the world if he's not at all interested in you? We also see that Joe and Carl make a deal for

Joe to help Jimmy, though, as we've seen, Jimmy's won almost half of the races he's driven in.

But when Joe arrives, he's a flat character already. In other words, he's someone whose character appears to be rather unchangeable. We know he used to be a race driver, retired after or because of a crash in which Brandenberg was almost killed, and has only returned now because his former boss, Carl, wants him back.

Joe and Carl Meet in Toronto

It's odd that when Joe returns, he's under the impression that Carl wants him to be a driver, but Carl is under the impression that Joe will be Jimmy's mentor. That begs yet another question: Why the confusion? This agreement should have been negotiated before Joe came to Canada, not after. When told the news, Joe initially says he won't do it, but Carl says you owe me (though we don't know why) and, without a fight, without engaging in any kind of positive conflict, Joe stays.

Joe's then introduced to a couple of men who are representatives of the car's sponsors (one of whom says he thought Joe was dead) and to Lucretia Jones (aka Luke) (Stacy Edwards) who is with the team for a year(!) doing an "exposé on male dominance in racing." Unfortunately, that's a kind of misplaced "McGuffin." An *exposé* is meant to expose something that hasn't been exposed. It's a well-known fact that men have always dominated the sport of Formula One racing, so what exactly is she exposing? Obviously, she's there as a potential love interest for Joe who, as we find out, is divorced.

In practice, Joe does the three-coin trick (i.e., gets his rear tire to pick up three coins on the track), which shows how he hasn't lost any driving skill over the years. Then, at Carl's prompting, he walks over to Jimmy to set up a meeting to discuss "strategy."

First Encounter with Jimmy

At that point, DeMille enters the scene and informs Joe in no uncertain terms that he needs to "channel" through him. That's the beginning of a potential conflict, but begs the question: Why? Carl, the car's owner, has hired Joe to mentor Jimmy and he's just told him to talk to the kid, so what's that got to do with Jimmy's brother? Nothing. DeMille's intervention not only undermines the potential success of the team, but also undermines his own greedy ambitions since Joe has been hired to tutor Jimmy which would, presumably, help everyone.

In a series of crosscuts, we see Jimmy at a disco somewhere in Toronto. In the meantime, Joe is playing pool with Luke who, it seems, is only interested in being with Joe rather than doing her exposé, but no one seems to care. Jimmy sees Sophia at the disco (apparently, the only disco in Toronto) and the scene shows the two of them "on target" to become lovers.

The next day in the garage area we meet Cathy (Gina Gershon), Joe's ex. According to Cathy, Joe left her and she married Memo, the other driver on the team, whom Joe has now replaced. Sophia, dumped by Brandenberg, has now changed allegiances and is also in the garage area looking for Jimmy. Just as an aside here. Automobile racers have been (and still are) some of the most superstitious athletes in the world. Some of their superstitions include, or have included, the following:

- Place no peanuts on the radiator of a car.
- Don't wear anything new before a race.
- Always get into the car on the same side with the same foot.
- Avoid the color green at all cost.

- Don't use the same pit stall in a race in which you've had a prior accident.
- Don't, under any conditions, allow women into the garage area before a race.

Clearly, the last rule has been violated in *Driven*. So either the superstition has disappeared or superstitions weren't important to begin with or, now that women drive, the superstition has no standing, but in any case, what is missing here are the superstitions that these particular drivers have. Stallone seems to be interested in trying to capture something of the *reality* of Formula One racing, yet one of the most critical things about racing is superstition and that detail, which could be critical in developing a character, plays no part in the film.

Second Encounter with Jimmy

So, for no apparent reason, Joe replaces Memo who doesn't seem too disturbed about being replaced and before the race, Joe says to Jimmy, "Good luck." Up to this point, Joe's neither done nor said anything of consequence to help Jimmy out. Jimmy's usually been by himself working on his laptop as if it were a video game, watching races on television or practicing on some racing software. There has been no strategy set for the race by either Joe or Carl and neither of them have any idea what their responsibilities are for the upcoming race other than to drive around in loops.

During the race, there's an accident. At that point, Carl radios Joe to come into the pits as Jimmy and Brandenberg fight for the lead. It's a maneuver that Carl has planned. He times the pit stop so that Joe leaves the pits at the same time the two lead cars pass by and by running "interference" for Jimmy, Jimmy wins. The problem here is that Jimmy could have won without Joe's help; that is, the maneuver could have been accomplished by Memo as

well as Joe since it was Carl's idea in the first place. It had nothing to do with skill. Until that time, Joe hasn't mentored Jimmy
at all, so why did Carl need him in the first place? The fact that
Joe confronts Carl after the race and says, "Don't do that again,"
doesn't make sense either. Joe has been contracted by Carl to be
Jimmy's partner. Jimmy is the lead car and Joe's job is to comple-
ment Jimmy, nothing else. So what's the problem?

After the press conference, Joe comes to talk to Jimmy.

Third Encounter with Jimmy

This is their third encounter, but once again DeMille intervenes
and repeats that if Joe wants to talk to Jimmy he should talk to
him first. Jimmy says nothing and Carl, the person from whom
everyone should be taking orders, can't be found. The following
situations bring up some major flaws in character development
and conflict, as well as plot:

1. We know Joe's job is to mentor Jimmy, yet Jimmy's
   brother, DeMille, constantly interferes with that job.
2. Carl has told Joe that he's to assist Jimmy, yet Joe is pissed
   off because Carl asked him to pull into the pits and play
   interference to enable Jimmy to win. But that's his job.
3. A number of encounters could have presented positive
   conflict, but they don't get played out:
   • Joe versus DeMille
   • Joe versus Carl
   • Carl versus DeMille
   • Joe versus Memo
   All of these potentially positive conflictual scenes are
   neutralized because nothing of substance occurs. Joe's
   attitude in each of the situations is passive.
4. Jimmy's character is absolutely stagnant because he doesn't
   say anything and allows his brother to do the talking for

him. Joe's character is also stagnant because he can't do the job he's supposed to do, so as a mentor, Joe is useless. If Joe is the hero here, then there isn't a point of departure, and as a character study, Joe hasn't changed nor is he likely to change. If Jimmy is the hero here, then his character has been passive and remains passive. His brother dominates and Jimmy, who should know better, merely acquiesces.

Jimmy, DeMille, Sophia

Sophia is now Jimmy's partner, but still all DeMille can talk about is money. The odd thing about DeMille is that even though he is Jimmy's manager, everything he does tends to undermine what Carl wants to do. As a matter of fact, during the entire film and in terms of conflict, there is never a face-to-face situation between Carl and DeMille that would help validate certain points or add to their characters. That void is a major flaw in the film.

Japan is the next race. At a hotel swimming pool, we see Jimmy still working at the computer and he asks Sophia, who is now his "steady squeeze," how Brandenberg does it—win, that is. She answers, "Focus." It's an odd question coming from a driver who is actually tied for the world championship and, by virtue of that fact, is doing exceptionally well, but let's buy it. What follows is a very odd scene, especially in terms of character development, in which Joe has a talk not with Jimmy, but with Beau Brandenberg!

Joe Talks with Beau

Joe tells Beau to take her, Sophia, back. Suddenly, Beau's not sure he did the right thing. Joe gives him some fatherly advice— crawl back to her. Apparently, those words of wisdom prompt Beau to ponder his earlier decision. Of course, we never know exactly why Beau cut off the relationship in the first place. But what's odd here is that Joe seems to be more like Beau's mentor than Jimmy's. As a matter of fact, Joe has had nothing of substance to say to Jimmy in the film, yet in this scene he's befriending his chief rival. Curious.

Joe and Luke as an Item

This brief scene is meant to show how solid Joe's relationship with Luke is by advancing their respective characters; however, during it, Joe merely mumbles. He's able to spit out a few words of dialogue and then the scene cuts away to a series of crosscuts of the night before the race with Brandenberg training while Jimmy parties and Sophia ponders her future.

The Japan Race, Cathy in the Pits

The scene then shifts to the race in which Jimmy slams into the wall and loses. But once again, there has been no clear strategy set by anyone involved with the team. What's odd about this accident is that he just won the previous race in Toronto, but apparently he hasn't learned anything. The fact that he's a rookie is irrelevant. No one seems to be able to connect with him; he seems incapable of learning anything new, yet he's still in contention for the world championship! The Japan race is supposed to be Race 14 which would leave only six more races; however, as we'll see, there are only three races left. What happened to the other races is a mystery lost in the pages of the script.

From Japan we're suddenly thrust back to Chicago at a black-tie formal party being held to exhibit new Formula One prototypes. Joe, of course, dresses casually either because he's different or because Stallone refused to wear formal attire. Regardless, Cathy shows up and makes some crude comments to Joe and Luke. Luke, of course, is about as much of a journalist as Joe is and any pretexts she had regarding her journalism duties have been abandoned. The few questions she asks are painfully superficial, lack any intelligence, and have nothing to do with her assignment which, as we know, was to expose male dominance in auto racing. Luke, who is plain, warm, and cuddly, is cast merely as a counterpoint to Cathy who is extremely sexy, rude, and hostile. The contrast between them leads to a potential conflict in the bathroom scene.

Cathy and Luke

We can dismiss the fact that the dialogue between them is gratuitous; it tends to maintain Cathy's "bitchy" character making her seem even less attractive than she had been. But why she should be rude to Luke is puzzling. One would think she'd be warning her about Joe since the implication is that Joe was a wife abuser (manhandled her) before he dumped her; however, Luke doesn't ever say, "Hey, I'm just a journalist writing an exposé about F1 racing." She merely plays as if she's Joe's girl and halfheartedly defends Joe even though she knows absolutely nothing about him.

Jimmy is there coupled with Sophia, but Brandenberg is there as well. While Jimmy is being interviewed, Sophia slips silently away and begins talking to Beau. Jimmy leaves in mid-interview and gets in between the two of them. Suddenly, DeMille arrives, attempting to defuse potential trouble. Joe senses an upcoming skirmish, but does absolutely nothing to break it up.

Beau and Jimmy Clash, the Chase

DeMille drags Jimmy away as Beau offers Sophia the ring she left back in Australia. She takes it and becomes his "item" again but not before Beau and Jimmy almost come to blows; Joe, who sees what's been going on, still does nothing. This situation leaves the viewer in a quandary. Joe is Jimmy's partner yet Joe has encouraged Beau to take Sophia back. Sophia appears to be a groupy and has no real allegiances to anyone. Whomever is convenient at the time seems to be the man of her choice.

Apparently this abrupt breakup is too much for poor Jimmy to handle and out of anger Jimmy steals one of the prototype cars off the showroom floor. That stupidity is immediately followed by another as Joe steals another prototype and goes after him. Somehow both of them get out without hurting anyone and Joe begins chasing Jimmy through the streets of downtown Chicago. The chase, of course, has absolutely nothing to do with either the story or with character development.

What's clear about this film is that whenever there is a need for a character to be developed, we get a chase/race scene. As a matter of fact, I would guess that, in the entire 109 minutes of the film, at least 40 percent of it is taken up with establishing and/or cutting to shots of the various venues and/or racing sequences, none of which demand dialogue or character development. Besides the obvious fact that they couldn't have started the cars in the first place (Formula One race cars cannot be started with a key!), besides the fact they could have endangered the lives of a number of innocent people, besides the fact they destroyed property, the chase only advances Jimmy's character as being an irresponsible and rather psychotic person. He's definitely not the kind of person you want driving a car worth hundreds of thousands of dollars. When the chase finally ends, it then becomes an argument between Joe and Jimmy. What do they argue about? Sophia.

Joe and Jimmy: After the Chase

It would appear that they could have had that simple little chat without the chase. But it's only here, about halfway through the film, that Joe becomes Jimmy's mentor and apparently changes Jimmy's view of life by simply stating that a person can accomplish anything if he has the "will and faith." If this dialogue sounds a lot like Rocky's, you know why. Suddenly, Jimmy has a *midpoint epiphany*—an epiphany a main character has about midway through a film—and has "learned something." Just what he's learned is unclear, but Joe says by the end of the "season" Jimmy should know "what he's made of." Joe also gives Jimmy some kind of trophy that Joe won many years ago and, apparently, Jimmy is touched by the gift.

The next scene (which should actually be the two of them standing in court wearing orange jumpsuits and handcuffs) has them flying on a private jet discussing "strategy" with spoons as Luke, who says nothing, participates in their collective happiness. Apparently, they're now on their way from Chicago to Germany.

We also discover there are only two races left in the season: Germany and Detroit. Even though after the race in Japan there were supposed to be six, but who's counting? We also discover that Joe and Jimmy have been fined $25,000 by the racing commissioner. Who cares? They broke city, state, and federal laws and without stretching our imagination would have been released on a huge bond or be in jail, but facts aren't that important here.

We find out too that Brandenberg leads in the point totals by four, with Jimmy in second place. For the first time in the film, we see Jimmy and Joe talking together without DeMille's interference. Why DeMille isn't there is curious since he's always come between them before and, since he hasn't been told by Carl not to interfere, the lack of his presence is curious. When DeMille does show up, instead of making a statement, he asks Jimmy: "You don't have to come to me anymore?" Apparently not and DeMille leaves.

At this point, Jimmy seems to be cheerful and relaxed and Joe kisses Luke's hand as a way of letting us know they're more romantically involved even though he hasn't laid either a finger or a lip on her yet. We get numerous dissolves between Joe and Jimmy as Joe is seemingly tutoring Jimmy and Jimmy seems eager to listen. After all this help, we get the following odd discussion.

Carl and Joe Talk About Jimmy

Seemingly out of nowhere, Carl suddenly believes Joe is better with Jimmy off the track rather than on it (though there's been no proof of that) and says Memo will drive in the German race instead of Joe. In terms of plot development, this decision makes absolutely no sense because there's nothing to indicate Memo would do better than Joe in this race. To the contrary, Joe would be better by virtue of the fact that Jimmy now trusts him and they've presumably worked on strategy together. Likewise, given Joe's background, he would probably be a better driver in the rain, a detail that's been shoved down our collective throat on numerous occasions. Carl also tells Joe that if Jimmy doesn't deliver next time out (i.e., win this time) he (Jimmy) goes (i.e., he's fired) and so does Joe.

Of course, that seems to be a ludicrous comment to make in light of what's been happening. It's clear that Jimmy's attitude has mildly improved since Joe's arrival even though there's really been very little evidence to support why. Apparently, much of it was due to Joe's one-minute lecture on "will and faith," which made all the difference, although that "speech-oid" in itself is not a very convincing bit of dialogue.

In the next scene, Joe, Jimmy, and Luke (who by now has abandoned any pretense of being a journalist—she has no tape recorder, no notebook) sit together having lunch as Jimmy explains strategy to a seemingly preoccupied Joe. At the same time, Memo is in his room putting a crucifix around his neck and crossing himself which more than likely means he's: (a) going to get into an accident and/or (b) going to get killed.

Jimmy and Memo in the Garage

Now it's race day. Cathy is in the garage (recall the superstitions), but Joe ignores her sarcastic comments yet again. Throughout this little exchange, all Jimmy and Memo say to each other is: "Be safe." Be safe? That's a bit like saying to someone going out into a rainstorm: "Don't get wet." Not only is it painfully obvious, but it's painfully immaterial. Clearly, the statement is meant to be a foreshadowing, but beyond that there is and has been no strategy set up between them nor between them and Carl! The only specific advice is given by Carl at the beginning of the scene in which he admonishes Memo not to drive "his own race," which he's done in the past, but to drive the team's race. But by the end of the scene, Cathy's telling Memo how he's going to win. So what's that all about?

The German Race

The next scene is in Brandenberg's pits as he's dealing with some strange woman who's made a bet that she can kiss all the drivers. She starts to kiss him, Beau stops her and tells her "she's lost," but "see me next year." Apparently that gesture is meant to show how "committed" Beau is to Sophia but, once again, who cares?

The fact that this is the second-to-last race is reemphasized, and we see yet again that there's a threat of rain, which in itself has become a major "character" in the film. Before the race, Beau and Jimmy apologize to each other and there's a very brief scene between Joe and Jimmy in which the former tells the latter, "Stay in your world, not his." He might just as well have said, "Don't take your hands off the steering wheel." Yet again, the words are somewhat meaningless because they would be irrelevant to a driver who's already won as many races as Jimmy has.

The race begins and, predictably, the rain comes, but it doesn't just rain, it pours. It's raining so hard that it's impossible to drive because it's not possible to see; however, for some very strange reason (which would actually have heightened the tension), the officials don't stop the race—hard to believe. It's patently obvious that for driver safety the officials would have at least temporarily postponed it, which happens a lot in auto racing. After all, they do it in baseball and that's not a very life-threatening sport (unless you're on steroids).

Predictably, there is a major accident, but, contrary to all racing protocol, there's no yellow flag! The racers just keep racing as if nothing has happened. Suddenly, to Carl's consternation, Memo unilaterally decides to run "his own race," not the team's—exactly what Carl told him not to do. Cathy, who's in the pits with the rest of the team, cheerfully encourages Memo to "win," which is exactly what Carl doesn't want. The team demands that Memo back off, but Cathy continues to encourage him to forge ahead. Predictably, as well, Memo goes into a skid and, in the "mother of all crashes," flies into the air and lands in some lake not even close to the track. Still there's no yellow flag, let alone a red one, and the race goes on.

In a feat of monumental stupidity, Jimmy turns his car around and, driving against traffic, rushes to his sunken teammate! In another equally stupid action, Brandenberg, too, stops his car to help rescue Memo. So we've got two drivers trying to help another driver; we've got the medics still on their way; and with all the chaos that's occurring, the race is still going on! Finally, the rescue team arrives, but only after Memo's been saved by the two drivers. Of course, in terms of dramatic potential, the scene is supposed to do the following:

1. Bond Beau and Jimmy
2. Set up a final competition between Beau and Jimmy
3. Bring Joe back into the picture for the final race

Obviously, we have to forget the fact that it's not at all realistic, but it does tend to set up a kind of "Rocky on wheels" ending, which is the kind of motif that Stallone has constantly tried to reproduce over almost a third of a century.

Predictably, Memo survives and is recuperating in the hospital. Jimmy is there as well because of an injured foot sustained during the rescue and Brandenberg, who was unhurt, arrives at the hospital with Sophia. He says to Jimmy that he didn't want to win the championship that way (i.e., with Jimmy out of the competition). While that scene is going on, Joe is in the garage looking over Jimmy's mangled car. Suddenly, Carl shows up and gives us the bad news.

Joe and Carl in the Garage, Jimmy

For some reason, Carl says he's going to terminate Jimmy's contract; however, this decision doesn't make much sense for two reasons: (1) Jimmy saved a fellow driver's life and thereby gave up the chance to win the world championship as a rookie; and (2) Brandenberg also lost the race so they're in the exact same place as they were before the race.

The confrontation with Carl and Joe is very interesting in terms of character and conflict. It's a situation in which the older racer, apparently the wiser racer, gives us some insight into the character of the other racer. It's a scene that's very reminiscent of the confrontation in *Rocky* between Mickey and Rocky after Rocky lost his locker to another boxer. Similarly, Carl, like Mickey, shows some emotion in the scene as Joe, like Rocky, merely stands there patently emotionless. In terms of character development, Joe, if he's supposed to be the main character, hasn't really learned anything and therefore his character has not altered. What this scene does do, however, is set up the final race, a race for Joe to prove something to himself. We also discover the fact that under Carl's orders DeMille (who's not paid attention to Carl for the entire film) has sold out his own brother and is trying to sign Brandenberg for the next racing season.

While Jimmy is working on his laptop (something he seems to do all the time), DeMille tells him he's going to a meeting. We know, but Jimmy doesn't, that his own brother is selling him out. In terms of character development, DeMille is merely out for himself and has absolutely no ethics. Jimmy might just as well be a stranger.

Feeling guilty, Sophia calls Jimmy to tell him about "the deal" his brother is trying to cut and, somehow, Jimmy limps out and confronts DeMille outside the hotel. Just how he got there is a mystery as is how he knew where his brother would be.

Jimmy and DeMille: The Confrontation

The confrontation between the two is not very convincing. DeMille says he's been working with Jimmy for ten years (that would have made Jimmy about fifteen when he started racing which is highly unlikely) and he resents the fact that Jimmy sold himself out to the has-been (i.e., Joe). In terms of the storyline, that statement doesn't make sense because Joe was hired by Carl to help Jimmy. Jimmy didn't sell out his brother, Carl hired Joe to help him. So it would have been in DeMille's best interest to work *with* Joe instead of *against* him, which he's done throughout the film. In terms of character development, it merely continues DeMille's character as being egotistic, selfish, and greedy and Jimmy's character as being painfully passive. All of these fabricated conflicts between DeMille and Jimmy or DeMille and Joe are neutral conflicts that aren't really conflicts at all. What's worse is that they keep being repeated without any change in content.

Finally, we get to the climactic race in Detroit. Before the race begins, Brandenberg backs out of the deal with DeMille and DeMille gets slapped in the face by Sophia. Just why Beau backed out is unclear. Perhaps, in a moral dilemma, Sophia blackmailed him sexually. So it's all come down to this final race of the season and, presumably, what Joe will finally tell Jimmy will be of critical importance. After all, this is it. If Jimmy wins, he wins the championship; if he loses, he loses everything.

Joe and Jimmy

Joe tells Jimmy he knew about the deal with his brother but wanted them to work it out, which they didn't. Joe also reiterates what he said in Chicago—by the end of the season, win or lose, Jimmy will know what "he's made of." Well, it's the end of the season. Of course, Joe told that to him in Chicago which was immediately before the German race, the second-to-last race of the season. How's that happen? So Joe now challenges Jimmy to show what "he's made of," exactly what he said before. Apparently, Joe's mentoring skills have severe limitations since the best he can do in any situation is merely repeat himself. But that's not where it ends.

The Last Race

At that point, Jimmy asks Carl to let him drive; however, he doesn't say it with passion, but like someone asking for a favor. Carl concedes, but only if Jimmy can pass two tests: (1) the "rule" that no driver can drive unless he can get out of the car in five seconds, and (2) Carl's vertical test—hopping on his injured foot ten times. Besides the fact that hopping ten times is arbitrary, there are several reasons why the second test is patently stupid.

1. Jimmy is one win away from a world championship because Brandenberg didn't finish in Germany either, so they're still tied.
2. If Jimmy wins, there are riches and celebrity for everyone.
3. By having Jimmy jump on his foot, he'll only aggravate the injury thus undermining his chances of winning for himself and the team.

Perhaps there's some minor dramatic potential here, but really there's nothing significant. Having Jimmy jump ten times on his injured foot (whether or not it's an F1 rule) isn't going to make an audience shiver with excitement or stand up in the aisles and cheer after he does it because it's not like Rocky going the distance. It also makes Carl's character appear petty and stupid because it was Carl who initiated the entire mentoring process in the first place, and by forcing Jimmy to jump, he's not only undermining Jimmy's career but the team's chances of winning since we know Brandenberg is not in the picture.

Prior to the race, Jimmy thanks Sophia for calling him; Brandenberg tells Sophia he loves her and vice versa; and now that everyone is friends, it's time to race. At the beginning, Brandenberg is in fourth, Joe in tenth, and Jimmy in twenty-sixth position. Of course, there's the obligatory accident that damages Joe's front fender, which needs to be replaced—a situation that moves him back to twenty-seventh position next to Jimmy. In a stunning bit of creative teamwork (that neither one of them ever discuss prior to the race), the two somehow collaborate and in a series of rapid dissolves pass everyone else on the track.

With twenty laps to go, Jimmy is in seventh and Joe is in sixth. There's another accident. No yellow, no red. Now they're in second and third behind Brandenberg. There's another pit stop and now they're in the final ten laps with Brandenberg in first, Jimmy in second, and Joe in third. Jimmy takes the lead over Brandenberg, then loses it with only three laps to go. Joe tries to "seize the moment" and moves into second place, then takes the lead himself, but backs off as Jimmy gains "courage" and overtakes Brandenberg to win by inches.

Suddenly, Luke, who's been missing most of the time, is back in the picture . . . literally. Also, and just as suddenly, Cathy, who's been watching the race with Memo from his hospital room, is happy that Jimmy's team won even though her husband could have been killed because he listened to her and didn't follow Carl's orders. Go figure.

Final Sequence

In the final sequence, Joe rushes to congratulate Jimmy, but not before Beau congratulates him. DeMille, who's standing in the audience, claps and smiles as if he's finally learned some lesson, but we can't imagine what. Jimmy holds up the winning *trophy*. Joe finds Luke in the crowd. Beau gets his trophy, Joe gets his, and Jimmy gives DeMille a smile as DeMille smiles back. All is forgiven and everyone is happy. The end. So what have we learned about character and conflict here? Let's begin with Joe.

Joe Tanto

Joe doesn't have a character arc. At the end of the film, the presumption is that he and Luke will get together since that's been alluded to (but poorly developed) throughout the course of the film. Yet no meaningful relationship has been established between them and the history of his marriage to Cathy is ambiguous at best. However, there are allusions to Joe's being an "abusive" husband and that he "left her," but the allegations are never confirmed. Why Cathy doesn't share that information with Luke is curious. She looks at Luke as a competitor when it's clear that she has nothing but disdain for Joe and appears to be very happily married to Memo. So there's no real change in Joe's character. What we have is not a character arc as we've talked about arcs, but a flatline. If Joe's not the main character, then he's not been a very good mentor either. Rather than having a presence at the outset of the film, or at least early in Act II, Joe says nothing of substance until the film is about 60 percent finished.

Jimmy Blye

Jimmy's arc is equally as confusing. He starts at the top, dips slightly, and returns to the top. It's not so much a character *arc* that he goes through as it is a character *dip*. This is the same sit-

101

uation we see in Jack Lucas' character in *The Fisher King*. He too starts at the top, then falls, but the major difference is there's a significant change in his character from being a successful radio personality to someone who wants to commit suicide. There is no such major change in Jimmy's character because there's no need for him to change.

The Others

The other supporting characters have their own problems. Carl's character is flat and often contradictory; DeMille is one-dimensional, purely out for himself; and all three women—Luke, Cathy, and Sophia—are cardboard characters with very little to say and very little to do.

Surprisingly, the only character who makes even the slightest change is not the hero! Brandenberg cuts off his engagement with Sophia (Greek for "wisdom"), has second thoughts about it after his chat with Joe, gets back together with her, and finally tells her he loves her. Convincing? No, but at least he makes the attempt.

If we take a look at the conflict charts, we see the following.

The *Driven* Character/Conflict Charts

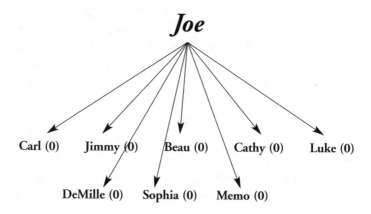

Joe

Carl (0)   Jimmy (0)   Beau (0)   Cathy (0)   Luke (0)

DeMille (0)   Sophia (0)   Memo (0)

Jimmy

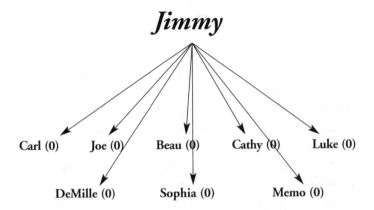

Joe really has neutral conflicts with everyone. His scenes with Jimmy don't advance any engaging kind of conflict whatsoever and with Beau they're not really conflictual at all. Joe essentially ignores both DeMille and Cathy, and he never really engages them in the conflictual issues at hand. Actually, he avoids confrontations with them, and Joe isn't in conflict at all with either Luke or Sophia. One can assume that Joe's in conflict with himself, but, that's never clearly defined.

Jimmy is also in neutral conflict with Carl, Beau, Joe, Sophia, and DeMille. He too is presumably in conflict with himself, but that isn't clearly defined either. So what's left is a series of interrelationships in which genuine conflict, as we've been talking about it, is absolutely missing.

Unlike Rocky, Joe Tanto doesn't seem to be that much in conflict with himself and for that reason suffers very little. That lack of an inner conflict results in a static character. Jimmy seems to be in conflict with himself, but even though there is a midpoint epiphany for him, it really doesn't alter his character arc. In other words, nothing appears about midway through the film that would alter the direction of his arc appreciably. In *Rain*

103

Man, Charlie's midpoint epiphany is when he learns who Raymond really is. Jimmy's midpoint epiphany (if we can call it that) is the cliché-ridden pep talk Joe gives him after the Chicago car chase and after Joe offers him the little toy trophy he won. Jimmy's backstory is never revealed; his relationship to his brother has no foundation; and though he appears somewhat dependent on his brother, it's for the pedestrian things in life (e.g., reserving an airline ticket—but since they fly in private jets, who cares?) and for handling promotion and publicity, which wouldn't be Jimmy's job in the first place.

Much of the problem with the script lies in the superficial characterization it gives these characters. We need to know the important things about Joe and Jimmy, but we never get them and what we do get doesn't make a lot of sense. Joe's lack of mentoring skills minimizes his role as a tutor, and if we look at the quest scheme, we get some interesting results. If it's Joe's story, there's a kind of a separation from his normal way of life, but no initiation and no return. By chance, Carl calls Joe, but there's no reluctance on his part. He goes. He works. He drives. There's no initiation because he's done all that before and in the end there's no return because he's the same guy at the end that he was in the beginning. Hence, there's been no dramatic revival in his character.

One might anticipate that, in some way, Luke would be Joe's emotional redeemer, but her character is so badly written, and their meetings so horribly unromantic and insignificant, that there's simply nothing to her. As a matter of fact, after the fiasco in Chicago we rarely see the two of them together and when we do, she says nothing (on the plane, at lunch) until the final race when Joe comes up to her in victory lane and says, "I'm glad you stuck around." To which she responds, "You were really something out there." She then goes on to say, "Go on, you're missing your celebration" and Joe says, "Don't go anywhere." She smiles at him twice. I know Adrian and Luke ain't no Adrian.

To be fair to Stallone, the script has the two of them returning to Joe's farm, which makes a lot more sense. As a matter of fact, the script begins and ends with them at the farm, which fits in better with the Aristotelian scheme of things; however, for whatever reason, director Renny Harlin felt otherwise since there's no room for Aristotle in crash scenes.

One of the main questions, if not *the main* question, one needs to ask is: What's Joe's purpose? If it's meant to be his story, we never see him in his normal environment; he doesn't question his ability to return; he has no mentor himself, though Luke could have accomplished that; and there is no road of trials for him to endure and overcome since he's been there before.

If this is Jimmy's story, there's no separation from where he came from. There is an initiation, of sorts, but no return. In the beginning of the story, he's a winner and at the end he's a winner. Even when he loses he still wins. We never see where he came from; we know nothing of his background; we never see him in his normal environment, and we never see what he had to endure to get to the top. We never see him suffer to achieve anything since, when we meet him, he's already a successful driver. It would have made more sense to have seen Jimmy rise to the top. Successful Formula One drivers don't begin as Formula One drivers; they have to struggle and come from somewhere to get to someplace.

What we do see are racing venues. As a matter of fact, outside of Joe's farm, almost every single scene shows a racing venue. With the exception of the showroom in Chicago, a disco, a pool, and hotel and hospital rooms, practically every scene shows racing, so we get no real sense of what these characters do at other times. Granted the crash scenes are spectacular, but there's little time for mourning dead or injured drivers or even thinking about the crashes since the players are so preoccupied with the petty relationships between and among the characters.

In the end, we're left with a film that obscenely lauds product placements, and reduces character and storyline to something that is merely there for appearances. The real star of the film is Formula One racing, which is a whole lot more exciting than the film we watched.

Amélie

Now that we've seen one good American movie and one not so good in relation to character development, where do we go from here? *Le Fabuleux Destin d'Amélie Poulain* presents us with a unique opportunity to apply everything we've been talking about in terms of character to a non-American feature film. The title of the French film was translated into English as *Amélie of Montmarte.* Just why that decision was made is curious since a more accurate translation would have been *"The Fabulous Destiny of Amélie Poulain,"* which would better serve the storyline film and the main character of the film.

The opening of the film is unique in that it establishes a moment in time when Amélie (Audrey Tautou) was conceived and it does so in a very unique and captivating way. Clearly, the visual effects created by Alain Carsoux are as instrumental to the storyline as anything else. But as the credits roll, introducing us to Amélie, we discover a lot about her character as a child.

Opening

The film opens in Montmarte where Amélie was born. Not coincidentally, the Montmarte setting plays a major role in her life and, in effect, closes the film as well. There is also the juxta-position of death (the allusion to a funeral that has taken place) and life (Amélie's conception) and that death–life juxtaposition continues throughout the film.

What we see during the credits is that Amélie exhibits a kind of inquisitiveness, imaginativeness, and cleverness born of necessity since she was home-schooled by her mother who, like her father Raphaël Poulain (Rufus), was anal retentive and devoid of affection. The lack of affection from her father results in *him* diagnosing that she's got a heart defect, which con-tributes to her home isolation.

Amélie's forced isolation allows her a free rein to explore her imagination and that is clearly something that will continue as she "grows up." When her only friend, her pet goldfish, is released into nature, she's left utterly alone.

We also see that she has a strong notion of what is fair and what isn't as demonstrated by the scene in which a man accuses her of causing an accident while taking photos with her instant camera. When she realizes she didn't cause the accident, we see that Amélie is not above revenge and of enforcing her own kind of "magical justice." Disconnecting her antagonist's television antenna at the critical moments of a soccer game is just what he deserves, and she continues with that kind of justice later.

The fact that her mother dies as a result of someone else's suicide tends to isolate Amélie even more and, in a way, is one of the main factors that contributes to her tendency toward physical and emotional isolation. As a matter of fact, we see Amélie alone most of the time except when she's at work at the Deux Moulins.

When first we see her at work, we are also introduced to the cast of characters who not only play a major part in the execu-tion of the film's storyline but a major part in her character development. But before being introduced to them, we see the photos of "the mystery man" and Amélie dressed as Zorro, a figure that is not serendipitous.

Deux Moulins for the First Time

Whom do we meet there? Well, we meet the following motley characters: Suzanne (Claire Maurier), the loveless owner; Georgette (Isabelle Nanty), the hypochondriac tobacconist; Gina (Clotilde Mollet), a chiropractic waitress; Hipolito (Artus de Penguern), a failed writer; Joseph (Dominique Pinon), Gina's neurotic ex-boyfriend; and Philoméne (Armelle), the flight attendant for whom Amélie cat-sits and who is extremely instrumental in the story even though she actually plays a very minor role.

Outside of her work, Amélie does most everything alone: watching others watch movies, skipping stones, squeezing kernels of grain, cracking the sugar on *crème brûlée;* even when she makes love, her attention is somewhere else. It's not a surprise then to discover that she also lives alone although she is often intrigued by the Glass Man, Raymond Dufayel (Serge Merlin), the arthritic, old painter who lives downstairs and who spends his time copying the masters. Her creative imagination is constantly alluded to as evidenced by examples such as her wondering how many Parisian couples are experiencing orgasms at any particular time.

By now, we've seen Amélie in her normal environment; that is, where she works, with whom she associates, what her backstory is, and who she is now. What we need in order to get her on her quest is a blunder or chance. And what is that?

The Broken Tile Scene

As she hears the shocking news about Lady Di's death, Amélie drops the lid of the bottle she's holding. It rolls across the bathroom floor and smacks into the wall causing a piece of tile to loosen. She gets on her knees, pries the tile back, and peers behind the fallen stone to discover a tin box. When she opens it, she sees a collection of old photos and little boy's toys. At that point, she decides (implicitly) to go on a quest to discover who lived in her flat decades ago and to return the forgotten, but emotionally priceless, items. If this quest works out well, she says, she'll become a regular do-gooder.

So this quest of "doing good for others" continues to shape her character. In the process of searching for the owner of the box, she speaks with the concierge, Madeléine Wallace (Yolanda Moreau) who lives in the apartment building; she tells Amélie the tragic love story about how her husband left her for his secretary before he was accidentally killed in South America. Mrs. Wallace actually reads Amélie some correspondence and that simple act remains with Amélie and pays off later in the film.

We are then introduced to Collígnon (Urbain Cancellier), the grocer, and his assistant, Lucíen (Jamel Debbouze). Amélie likes Lucíen but Collígnon constantly verbally abuses him because he's slow-witted. Collígnon suggests that Amélie visit his mother who would know who lived in her flat in the 1950s. Amélie visits Collígnon's mother who gives her the name: *Bredodeau.* With that name in hand, she sets off on her quest.

In the subway, Amélie first sees the blind man (Jean Darie), then she sees Nino Quincampoix (Mathíeu Kassovítz) who will become her love interest and who, for some odd reason, is looking under one of the instant photo machines for something. At that point, we get the backstory about Nino before Amélie leaves him and then she sees her father who is painting his garden gnome, which he's put next to his wife's ashes as a kind of monument even though she hated it.

Back at the Deux Moulins for the second time, Amélie looks up the names in the phonebook in her quest to discover

Dominique Bredodeau. But after three unsuccessful attempts, she returns home and literally runs into Dufayel, who tells her the name she's looking for is not Bredodeau, but *Bretodeau*.

So we see that she's accidentally discovered her mentor and at the same time we find out a bit more about Dufayel's character and a parallel subplot of the mysterious girl in the Renoir painting. Dufayel hands her Bretodeau's address and, expanding her character as someone who does not do things in an orthodox way, Amélie attracts Bretodeau's (Maurice Bénichou) attention as he walks along the Rue Mouffetard by calling him on a pay phone. Bretodeau can't let the phone ring. What he discovers is that she has left his missing box there, which brings him to tears. In a subsequent scene, Bretodeau is having a drink, discussing with the bartender (and an overhearing Amélie) the mystery of destiny and how this discovery has made him reconsider reconnecting with his family.

Immediately after her success with Bretodeau, she sees the blind man again, grabs his arm, and as they rush around the streets of Paris, she tells him what he can't see. Amélie now feels an overwhelming kind of harmony within.

One might think that she's finished her quest, but she hasn't. Her quest is to do good for others, but implied in that do-good notion is doing good for herself, and only when she's accomplished that will her quest conclude triumphantly. That situation is clearly manifest when she watches television alone in her bed and realizes how quickly life passes.

Her Life in Black and White

Here (in a kind of homage to *Zadig*) she watches her life as a black-and-white documentary while she questions what she's going to do or not do with it. Subsequently, she returns to her father's house and steals the garden gnome. We have no idea at that time what she plans to do with the gnome, but given her mischievous character, she's probably planning something unorthodox. Returning home after spending the night in one of the photo booths in a the subway station, she sees Nino for the second time at the Gare de L'Est.

Nino, Amélie, and the Mystery Man

Nino is more concerned with rushing after the mystery man (Marc Amyot) than he is with meeting Amélie. On the other hand, Amélie rushes after Nino and recovers a photo album that has fallen off his scooter as he chases the mystery man. She returns home with the album and peruses it. What's of interest here is that for Amélie the album, which is a collection of torn photos that have been glued together, becomes the replacement for Nino. At the same time, the photos tell us a lot about who Nino is and how much the two of them are alike.

Back at Deux Moulins for the third time, we hear Suzanne's sad love story and then Amélie begins to set up a relationship between Georgette and Joseph.

Amélie, Georgette, and Joseph at the Deux Moulins

This has now become Amélie's raison d'être: doing good for others—that's her quest and she continues on it quite happily. What she does in this situation is to make both Georgette and Joseph believe that the other one has an amorous interest. She does this kind of matchmaking very effectively.

We also see that her relationship with Dufayel continues in a way that perpetuates his role as her mentor. With the introduction of Dufayel's obsession with the mysterious girl in Renoir's painting (Colozine dei Canottieri) and the fact that after twenty years he still can't get the girl's face right, one of the major subplots in the story is revealed; that is, that Amélie associates herself with the character in the painting and tries to explain the possible psychological reasons why Dufayel can't get her right.

Subsequently, and almost by accident, Amélie reads a newspaper article about some missing letters that were found after a plane crash. At this point, the article seems insignificant, but, like every other "serendipitous event" in the film, it's not.

For the second time, we see Collígnon verbally abuse Lucíen, and instead of returning Collígnon's key, which Amélie had found still in his door, she makes a copy of it before replacing it.

We return to the Deux Moulins for the fourth time and see that the relationship between Georgette and Joseph is heating up which is exactly what Amélie hoped for.

For the third time, we see Collígnon abuse Lucíen. This time, however, Amélie has had enough of it and takes matters into her own hands. While Collígnon is working, she enters his apartment to do some damage. What she doesn't know is that Dufayel sees what she's doing from his apartment.

Collígnon's Apartment

Once in Collígnon's apartment, she alters reality in order to "get even" with Collígnon (e.g., replacing toothpaste with foot cream) and for mistreating Lucíen. At the end of her mischievousness, she pretends she's Zorro which is an allusion to the Zorro photo at the beginning of the film. The fact that she thinks of herself as Zorro is significant since the Zorro motif plays out later in the film.

The choice of Zorro is interesting because Zorro too attempted to right wrongs done to those marginal figures who could not fend for themselves. But, in addition, it's significant because his real persona was that of one who was least suspected of being Zorro. *Zorro*—Spanish for "fox"—is the story of a masked rider who battles the unjust rulers of the Los Angeles pueblo during the days of Spanish rule. His real identity is Don Diego de la Vega, son of a wealthy landowner, who returns from his studies in Spain to discover that Los Angeles is under the command of Capitan Monastario, a cruel man who relishes in the misuse of his power for personal gain. Don Diego adopts the secret identity of Zorro, a sinister figure dressed in black, and rides to fight Monastario's injustices. So, Amélie's choice of the Zorro disguise fits in perfectly with the Collígnon–Lucíen relationship and advances her character even more.

The Gnome and the Photos

Once again, Amélie visits her father who seems to be preoccupied and doesn't listen to anything she has to say. She naïvely questions him about the missing gnome and he hands her a photo of the gnome who's apparently in Moscow. What's marvelous about this subplot is that the garden gnome is, seemingly, on his own quest and this is the first of a series of photos that establishes that quest. The gnome's exploits are, of course, meant to prompt Amélie's father to do something with his own life: namely, travel.

Returning home, Amélie sees a number of posters plastered near the subway pleading for a return of *Lost Photos*. In the next scene, she's in her bedroom staring at the poster, which she's stuck on her mirror across from her bed; however, she takes no action relative to calling the phone number. This lack of action is in keeping with her character: inventive, but cautious. Clearly, if she calls the number, Nino's number, she will have to meet him and in the act of meeting him she will have to expose herself, which she is not eager to do.

Next, we get to see what's happened in Collígnon's apartment and how he has to "pay" for what he's done to Lucíen.

Deux Moulins for the Fifth Time

The following scene is the fifth scene at the Deux Moulins in which the relationship between Georgette and Joseph is reaching a feverish height. It's apparent not only by how they relate to each other, but by how her appearance has changed in terms of Georgette's hair, makeup, and so on. Juxtaposed with that scene we see Amélie finally calling the phone number on the poster, but when she discovers it's a porno palace, she thinks the worst and hangs up.

The subsequent scene is Lucíen bringing food as well as a video to Dufayel. The video, found under his mat, shows a horse running ahead of a pack of cyclists. Dufayel seems confused about where it came from and why he got it, but the allusion may be to the fact that "one can do whatever one wants to do regardless of obstacles."

Georgette and Joseph and the Photos

Back to the Deux Moulins for a sixth time where we get the pay-off of what Amélie has set up between Georgette and Joseph.

It's not coincidental that the next scene has Dufayel, Amélie's mentor, telling her that she should go see the boy at the porno store; she does so and is told by one of his co-workers that he's a "dreamer." She gives Amélie a brief history of the kinds of things Nino likes to do. Amélie doesn't leave the album there but, instead, takes it with her to the Fun Fair where Nino also works.

Amélie, the Skeleton, and the Montmarte Carousel

Amélie goes to the fair and pays for an eerie boat ride. What's exceptionally revealing about this scene is the brilliant juxtaposition of Amélie with the Skeleton who appears in her boat (who, presumably, is Nino) and how the skeleton moves and acts not in any terrifying way, but in a very seductive way. This action is not coincidental since it too will pay off later. When Nino is done for the day, he discovers a note about meeting someone at the Montmarte Carousel to get his album.

What's of interest here is the extent to which Amélie goes in order *not* to meet Nino. This action is clearly in character. From her surreptitious phone call to wearing sunglasses to having him see her at a distance, each action continues to both validate and layer her character. In other words, she's attracted by the game of "hide and seek" but petrified to get intimate with Nino. Nino then finds his album with yet another note about meeting. This is all part of her plan (as well as her quest) to meet him and yet it validates her reluctance to meet him. There's another letter from the gnome who is now in New York.

Amélie sneaks into Mrs. Well's apartment and takes her letters. At this point, we're not sure why, though in a previous scene we found out about the plane crash and the correspondence that was found there.

Deux Moulins and Collignon's Apartment Again

We're back at the Deux Moulins for the seventh time with Georgette and Joseph still infatuated with each other and that scene is juxtaposed with Nino at the porno palace asking his co-worker what Amélie looks like. We often see these kinds of juxtapositions in the storyline between the A-plot (i.e., Amélie's quest) and the other B-plots (e.g., Georgette and Joseph).

In the following scene, once again Collígnon abuses Lucíen and, for the second time, Amélie sneaks into Collígnon's apartment to avenge the abuse. Again, Dufayel sees what's going on.

The Letter and More

Subsequent to that scene, we see Amélie writing the fictional letter to Mrs. Wells based on the article she read; this eventually will close the circle to her (Mrs. Wells') love for her husband. Amélie cuts, pastes, photocopies, ages, and dries the letter. As Amélie spies on Dufayel, Dufayel spies on Amélie and sees what she's doing. At this point, it becomes fairly clear that Amélie intends to put an end to Mrs. Well's bitterness about her husband and, in effect, to get her to move on with her life.

We then get the last installment of Amélie's revenge on Collígnon, after which we see her discover Nino's posters that read "Where and When."

Amélie at the Gare de L'Est and Beyond

At the Gare de L'Est, we see Amélie taking her photo in her Zorro outfit at which point she also sees the bald-headed mystery man.

The following scene has Mrs. Wells receiving the "letter" from her dead husband and with that letter, she recovers her "lost" love and that particular subplot is ended.

There are more videos from Amélie to Dufayel and yet another photo from the garden gnome to Amélie's father. The gnome seems to be in Thailand. It's also here that we discover that it has been Philoméne, the flight attendant, who's been taking and sending the gnome's photos.

From Nino discovering Amélie's Zorro photo and the message to meet her at the Deux Moulins at 4 P.M. to the end of the film, every scene is absolutely integral to understanding Amélie's character.

Nino and Zorro to the End

Of course, Nino is ten minutes late and we get the brilliantly imaginative reasons why from Amélie's point of view; only Amélie could come up with these options. The first reason is very logical; the second is the reasoning of someone with a remarkable imagination, which we know she has. With Nino's arrival at the café, we can assume Amélie's obviously won her heart's desire, but she is still incapable of acting on it even though Nino's positive that he's uncovered "Zorro's secret identity." Still unable to confront her desires, Amélie collaborates with Gina to slip a note in Nino's jacket, which she does before he leaves. Unfortunately, the jealous and neurotic Joseph sees the action as well.

Once again, there's the juxtaposition of that scene and the following scene in which her dialogue with Dufayel deals with the girl in the Renoir painting. Again, she sees her life in a Zadigean black and white.

We also see Dufayel making his own videos before Amélie, now at the Gare de L'Est, calls about a broken photo machine that needs to be fixed.

Simultaneously, Nino discovers the note in his pocket and rushes to the station at which point he discovers the mystery man, now wearing red shoes, is merely the photo machine repairman! As Amélie starts to walk toward him, however, she's blocked by someone moving luggage and when he's passed by, Nino is gone. What's ingenious about this scene is how the notion of simultaneity plays here. Just as simultaneity opened the film, it continues within the film and, presumably, if

Aristotle is correct, will end the film thus linking the beginning with the end.

Subsequently, Nino returns to the Deux Moulins, a ninth scene there, looking for Amélie. She's not there, but he finds Gina.

The garden gnome has now returned home.

Gina and Nino leave and when Amélie returns, Joseph tells her a story about Gina and Nino that he fabricated based on circumstantial evidence, but Amélie believes it. Of course, that news disturbs her terribly so that when Mrs. Wells tells her about the letter she received before her husband died, Amélie isn't interested.

As she makes her famous plum cake, Amélie fantasizes about Nino and when Nino rings the door, she doesn't answer. The door is the barrier between them, between her and what she desires the most: love.

It's only after Nino leaves that she gets a phone call from Dufayel who tells her to go to her bedroom where she plays the video Dufayel made, in which he tells her to go after him.

When she opens the door again, Nino is there. What we see here is a kind of refrain from the Nino as Skeleton scene. As in the previous scene, there is no dialogue, but sensual and seductive touching and kissing that eventually leads the two of them into bed together as Amélie smiles and strokes his head.

So, at the end of the film, she's achieved her quest. She has returned with the *trophy* of love that she never had before.

The End Links to the Beginning

Not coincidentally, the film ends as it began with the alterations that we would have expected. We see closure to a number of the subplots that were initiated earlier: Hipolito's words scrawled on a wall; Bretodeau with his grandchild; Dufayel painting something other than Renoir's luncheon; and, finally, Amélie's father getting the point about living one's life as he heads to the international airport.

The ending, too, links with the beginning with the notion of simultaneity and with the idea that life itself is filled with minor and major discoveries.

In the very end, we see Amélie riding with Nino on his motorbike which also links with the beginning since Amélie was alone then and now she's not. The themes of life and death, of love lost then found, and of time passing are constant throughout the film and are augmented by the juxtaposition of individual things.

So all of the items we've been discussing in terms of character, quest, and conflict are exhibited in *Amélie*. Let's take a look at a character/conflict chart and what kinds of conflicts are in this film.

The *Amélie* Character/Conflict Chart

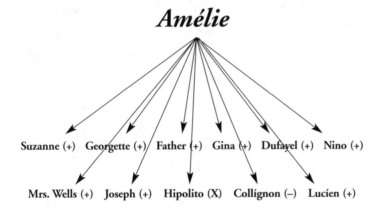

At the Deux Moulins

Amélie is not in conflict with anyone.

Suzanne is not in conflict with anyone.

Georgette is in negative conflict with no one, but eventually with Joseph.

Gina is in negative conflict with Joseph.

Joseph is in negative conflict with Gina, Hipolito, and eventually with Georgette.

Hipolito is in negative conflict with Joseph.

In the Apartment House

Mrs. Wells is initially in negative conflict with her husband, but that's resolved.

Dufayel is in positive conflict with Amélie.

Collígnon is in negative conflict with Lucién and Amélie.

Lucién is in negative conflict with Collígnon.

In Paris

Nino is in positive conflict with Amélie and with the mystery man.

In Conclusion

In the previous case studies, I've attempted to show that *conflict drives character*. The question arises, however, which kind of conflict is best? In *The Graduate*, Benjamin was in positive conflict with both Mrs. Robinson and Elaine even though the former could be considered a "negative" influence and the latter a "positive" one. In *Good Will Hunting*, Will was in positive conflict with Lambeau, Sean, and Skyler though the latter two had a greater influence on altering his character than the former. In *Driven*, Joe, if not Jimmy, seems to be in neutral conflict with practically everyone and that neutral conflict doesn't contribute to any substantial change. Finally, in *Amélie*, we see that she's in positive conflict with practically everyone! So which is better?

If we have to make some kind of judgment on the issue, I think it would be that we find varying degrees of conflict, and for there to be conflict doesn't necessarily mean that the characters have to scream and/or beat at each other. In each of the character-driven pieces (i.e., *The Graduate, Good Will Hunting, Amélie*), what we see are characters in positive conflict with themselves as well as with others in order to gain a better understanding of themselves. In other words, conflict can begin in a neutral way but eventually must move toward a positive one in the sense that the interrelationships between and among characters must do something to alter the fabric of the hero–protagonist. If the interrelationships are neutral, they prove futile and the main character remains static. Recall some of the films discussed here and you'll see how change (whether major or minor) was manifested in characters such as Benjamin, Will, Amélie, Conrad, Charlie Babbitt, Joe Buck, Babette, and so on. The reason for that alteration is because those characters are in films in which character plays a major role; in fact, character-driven pieces must rely on a significant degree of positive conflict.

Driven is not one of those films; clearly, it is a plot-driven story. If one is interested in Formula One racing and in high-tech crashes, it's the movie for you, but if you're interested in a film that explores intricate interrelationships between and among characters, the film goes nowhere. There are no changes (either minor or major) that affect Stallone's character or Pardue's character, or any other character for that matter, with the possible exception of Til Schweiger's character. Maybe that is the key reason that trying to come up with some conclusion to all of this is difficult.

Whether the hero–protagonist makes a minor change or a major change, the character, in some fashion, must be *affected by minor or major conflicts* that confront him or her. If those conflicts have no significant impact on the characters, there can be no significant change; if there is no significant change, then the characters have neither learned nor accomplished anything. If there's anything you can take with you at this point, that's what you need to take.

Appendix

Character/Conflict Analysis Exercises

You can use the following exercises to help in the shaping of character and conflict for your screenwriting.

1. Create a Character Summary
Create three columns. In the first column, list the characters' names; in the second column, list whether the character is the protagonist or antagonist and what his or her relationship is with the other characters; and in the third column, list the characters' motivation.

2. Create a Plot Summary
Create three columns. Label the first column: Beginning; the second column: Middle; and the third column: End. In each of the columns, decide what the focal plot point is. In other words, if there's a "love" plot at work, write what that love plot is. If there's a subplot at work, write what that subplot is.

3 Create a Sequence Summary

Create four columns. Label the first column: Time; label the second column: Beginning; the third column: Middle; and the fourth column: End. Then break the Time column into portions. For example, 0–20 minutes, 20–35, etc. This is meant to parallel the individual acts involved. In the columns you've created, summarize what's to happen.

4 Create a Scene Analysis

This is a bit more complex, but it can be helpful in understanding character and conflict. In the left column, list the minutes; in narrative, describe what's going to happen, in detail, during that particular minute; at the end of the scene, list the following three categories and describe exactly what fits:

- Conflict—the hero–protagonist versus who?
- Action—what is the focal point?
- Development—what happens in the scene that develops character?

As a test, choose a film you know well and apply these exercises to it before applying them to a work of your own.

Bibliography

Campbell, Joseph. 1972. *Hero with a Thousand Faces.*
Princeton: Princeton University Press.

Egri, Lagos. 1972. *The Art of Dramatic Writing.* New York:
Touchstone Books.

Frazer, Sir James George. 1995. *The Golden Bough.* New York:
Touchstone Books.

Gessner, Robert. 1970. *The Moving Image.* New York: E. P.
Dutton.

Goldman, William. 2000. *Which Lie Did I Tell?* New York:
Pantheon.

Lawson, John Howard. 1967. *Film, the Creative Process.* New
York: Hill and Wang.

Lucey, Paul. 1996. *Story Sense.* New York: McGraw-Hill.

Moore, Sonia. 1974. *The Stanislavski System.* New York:
Viking Press.

van Gennep, Arnold. 1961. *Rites of Passage.* Chicago:
University of Chicago Press.

Vogler, Chris. 1998. *The Writer's Journey: Mythic Structure for
Writers.* Los Angeles: Michael Wiese Productions.

Weston, Jessie. 1997. *From Ritual to Romance.* New York:
Dover Publications.